Contents

Parents' notes		2
1.	Place value	4
2.	Addition facts	6
3.	Subtraction facts	8
4.	Length	10
5.	Multiplication and division facts	12
6.	2D shapes	14
	TEST 1	16
7.	Time	18
8.	Fractions of shapes	20
9.	Addition	22
10.	Subtraction	24
11.	Sequences and patterns	26
12.	Comparing and ordering numbers	28
	TEST 2	30
13.	Rounding numbers	32
14.	Weight and mass	34
15.	3D shapes	36
16.	Multiplication	38
17.	Division	40
18.	Coordinates	42
	TEST 3	44
19.	Decimals	46
20.	Capacity	48
21.	Fractions of amounts	50
22.	Graphs	52
23.	Money	54
24.	Angles	56
	TEST 4	58
	Answers	60

Focus on Maths
Year 4
age 8 to 9

Text and illustrations © Hodder & Stoughton Educational 2004

First published 2004
exclusively for WHSmith by
Hodder & Stoughton Educational
338 Euston Road
London NW1 3BH

All rights reserved. Apart from any use permitted under UK copyright law, no part of this publication may be reproduced or transmitted in any form or by any means, electronic or mechanical, including photocopying, recording or any information storage and retrieval system, without permission in writing from the publisher.

Impression number   10 9 8 7 6 5 4 3 2 1
Year   2010 2009 2008 2007 2006 2005 2004

Text: Paul Broadbent and Peter Patilla

Typeset by Servis Filmsetting Ltd, Manchester

Printed and bound in Spain

A CIP record for this book is available from the British Library

ISBN 0 340 88772 9

Parents' notes

How this book can help your child

- This book has been written for children who are between 8 and 9 years old.
- It will support and improve the work they are doing at school, whichever maths scheme they use.
- The activities in the book have been carefully written to include the content expected of children at this stage in their development.
- The activities will help prepare your child for the different types of tests that occur in schools.
- The book offers support, development and challenge for all abilities.

Materials needed

- Pencil, coloured pencils, eraser and centimetre ruler.

Using the book

- There are 24 topics and 4 tests in the book. A test occurs after 6 topics have been completed.
- Each topic need not be completed in one session. Think of it as about a week's work.
- Do give help and encouragement. Completing the activities should not become a chore.
- Do leave out a specific topic until later should your child not have covered its content in school. The book has been written to support the teaching in school, not to pre-empt it.
- A calculator should not be used for the work in this book.
- Do let your child mark his or her own work under your supervision and correct any careless mistakes he or she might have made.
- When all the tests have been completed let your child fill in the Certificate of Achievement on the opposite page.
- Each double page has a title, explanation of the learning point, practice, extension and challenges.

Topic – the main learning point

Focus – helpful information and tips about the learning point

Practice – straightforward follow-up to the learning point

Extension – uses the learning point in a slightly different way

Challenge – takes the learning point further

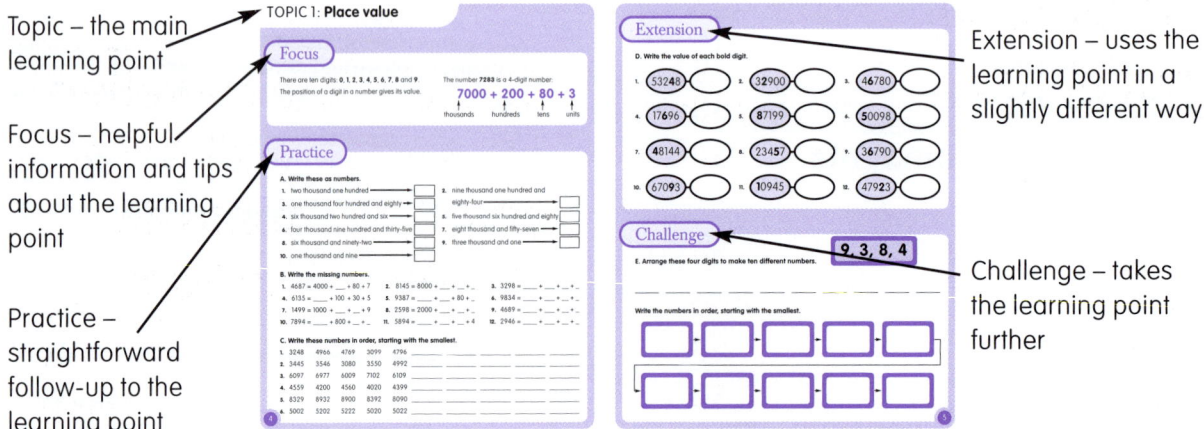

This certifies
that

_____

has completed

FOCUS ON MATHS YEAR 4

on _____

Scoring _____ on TEST 1

_____ on TEST 2

_____ on TEST 3

and _____ on TEST 4

TOTAL Score
out of 100 _____

40–50	good effort
50–60	well done
60–70	fantastic
70–100	brilliant

TOPIC 1: **Place value**

Focus

There are ten digits: **0**, **1**, **2**, **3**, **4**, **5**, **6**, **7**, **8** and **9**.
The position of a digit in a number gives its value.

The number **7283** is a 4-digit number:

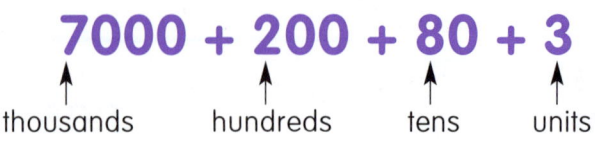

$$7000 + 200 + 80 + 3$$

thousands   hundreds   tens   units

Practice

A. Write these as numbers.

1. two thousand one hundred ⟶ ☐

2. nine thousand one hundred and eighty-four ⟶ ☐

3. one thousand four hundred and eighty ⟶ ☐

4. six thousand two hundred and six ⟶ ☐

5. five thousand six hundred and eighty ☐

6. four thousand nine hundred and thirty-five ☐

7. eight thousand and fifty-seven ⟶ ☐

8. six thousand and ninety-two ⟶ ☐

9. three thousand and one ⟶ ☐

10. one thousand and nine ⟶ ☐

B. Write the missing numbers.

1. 4687 = 4000 + ___ + 80 + 7

2. 8145 = 8000 + ___ + __ + _

3. 3298 = ____ + ___ + __ + _

4. 6135 = ____ + 100 + 30 + 5

5. 9387 = ____ + ___ + 80 + _

6. 9834 = ____ + ___ + __ + _

7. 1499 = 1000 + ___ + __ + 9

8. 2598 = 2000 + ___ + __ + _

9. 4689 = ____ + ___ + __ + _

10. 7894 = ____ + 800 + __ + _

11. 5894 = ____ + ___ + __ + 4

12. 2946 = ____ + ___ + __ + _

C. Write these numbers in order, starting with the smallest.

1. 3248   4966   4769   3099   4796   _____ _____ _____ _____ _____

2. 3445   3546   3080   3550   4992   _____ _____ _____ _____ _____

3. 6097   6977   6009   7102   6109   _____ _____ _____ _____ _____

4. 4559   4200   4560   4020   4399   _____ _____ _____ _____ _____

5. 8329   8932   8900   8392   8090   _____ _____ _____ _____ _____

6. 5002   5202   5222   5020   5022   _____ _____ _____ _____ _____

Extension

D. Write the value of each bold digit.

1. 5324**8** ⬭

2. 3**2**900 ⬭

3. 4**6**780 ⬭

4. 17**6**96 ⬭

5. **8**7199 ⬭

6. **5**0098 ⬭

7. **4**8144 ⬭

8. 234**5**7 ⬭

9. 3**6**790 ⬭

10. 670**9**3 ⬭

11. **1**0945 ⬭

12. 479**2**3 ⬭

Challenge

E. Arrange these four digits to make ten different numbers.

> **9, 3, 8, 4**

____ ____ ____ ____ ____ ____ ____ ____ ____ ____

Write the numbers in order, starting with the smallest.

TOPIC 2 : **Addition facts**

Focus

If you learn your addition facts, it can help with adding bigger numbers.

$$5 + 8 = 13$$
$$15 + 8 = 23$$
$$50 + 80 = 130$$

A quick way to add 9 is to add 10 and then take away 1:

$$14 + 9 \rightarrow 14 + 10 - 1 = 23$$

You can use this method to add 19 or 29:

$$+19 = +20 - 1 \qquad +29 = +30 - 1$$

Practice

A. Time how long it takes you to answer each block of sums. Try to beat your best time.

1.

3 + 8 =
4 + 6 =
5 + 9 =
7 + 4 =
8 + 8 =
3 + 9 =
6 + 5 =
9 + 9 =
4 + 8 =
7 + 7 =

2.

5 + 9 =
8 + 6 =
3 + 7 =
5 + 8 =
6 + 6 =
8 + 9 =
4 + 6 =
8 + 3 =
6 + 7 =
5 + 4 =

3.

14 + 5 =
12 + 7 =
16 + 9 =
11 + 5 =
13 + 8 =
18 + 7 =
14 + 8 =
12 + 6 =
19 + 5 =
17 + 7 =

4.

6 + 14 =
7 + 12 =
9 + 19 =
7 + 14 =
5 + 18 =
3 + 19 =
7 + 16 =
4 + 19 =
8 + 17 =
9 + 18 =

B. Write the missing numbers. Each pair must total 100.

1. 40 + ⬭

2. 60 + ⬭

3. 30 + ⬭

4. 70 + ⬭

5. 20 + ⬭

6. ⬭ + 50

7. ⬭ + 80

8. ⬭ + 10

9. ⬭ + 90

C. Write the answers.

1.
70 + 40 =
30 + 90 =
60 + 70 =
40 + 80 =
60 + 60 =

2.
90 + 40 =
60 + 50 =
80 + 70 =
90 + 50 =
70 + 70 =

3.
200 + 600 =
500 + 800 =
800 + 300 =
600 + 900 =
900 + 500 =

4.
500 + 300 =
300 + 800 =
400 + 700 =
700 + 600 =
900 + 800 =

Extension

D. Complete these addition patterns.

1.	2.	3.	4.	5.	6.
5 + 9 = _____	8 + 9 = _____	7 + 9 = _____	6 + 9 = _____	4 + 9 = _____	9 + 9 = _____
5 + 19 = _____	8 + 19 = _____	7 + 19 = _____	6 + 19 = _____	4 + 19 = _____	9 + 19 = _____
5 + 29 = _____	8 + 29 = _____	7 + 29 = _____	6 + 29 = _____	4 + 29 = _____	9 + 29 = _____
5 + 39 = _____	8 + 39 = _____	7 + 39 = _____	6 + 39 = _____	4 + 39 = _____	9 + 39 = _____
5 + 49 = _____	8 + 49 = _____	7 + 49 = _____	6 + 49 = _____	4 + 49 = _____	9 + 49 = _____

E. Write the answers.

1. Total 8 and 7

2. 900 plus 200

3. Add 40 to 50

4. Add 16 to 9

5. Total 6, 8 and 7

6. Increase 600 by 300

7. 40 plus 60

8. Add 19 to 8

9. 9 more than 52

10. Increase 38 by 3

11. Increase 130 by 40

12. Total 12, 9 and 6

13. 5 more than 21

14. 9 more than 25

15. 800 plus 400

Challenge

F. Look at the number machines.
Complete each table.

1.
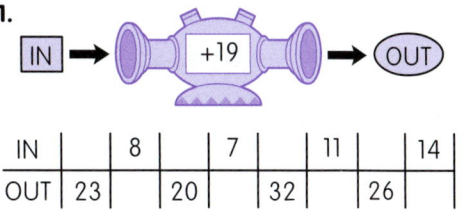

IN		8		7		11		14
OUT	23		20		32		26	

2.
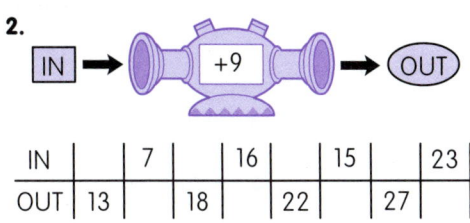

IN		7		16		15		23	
OUT	13		18		22		27		

3.
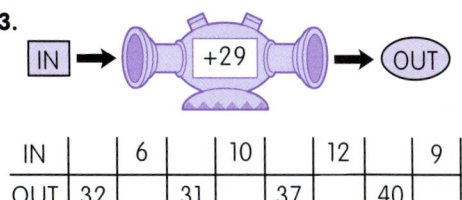

IN		6		10		12		9
OUT	32		31		37		40	

TOPIC 3 : **Subtraction facts**

Focus

If you learn your subtraction facts, it can help with taking away bigger numbers.

$$8 - 3 = 5$$
$$18 - 3 = 15$$
$$80 - 30 = 50$$

A quick way to take away 9 is to take away 10 and then add 1:

$$26 - 9 \longrightarrow 26 - 10 + 1 = 17$$

You can use this method to subtract 19 or 29:

$$-19 = -20 + 1 \qquad -29 = -30 + 1$$

Practice

A. Time how long it takes you to answer each block of sums.

Try to beat your best time.

1.

$17 - 6 =$
$15 - 8 =$
$16 - 9 =$
$13 - 5 =$
$18 - 7 =$
$19 - 4 =$
$14 - 6 =$
$15 - 9 =$
$18 - 5 =$
$17 - 9 =$

2.

$19 - 9 =$
$13 - 7 =$
$17 - 8 =$
$14 - 5 =$
$18 - 9 =$
$16 - 7 =$
$13 - 8 =$
$19 - 5 =$
$16 - 8 =$
$15 - 7 =$

3.

$24 - 8 =$
$27 - 4 =$
$26 - 9 =$
$22 - 5 =$
$23 - 6 =$
$28 - 7 =$
$24 - 6 =$
$29 - 8 =$
$21 - 5 =$
$27 - 9 =$

4.

$32 - 4 =$
$35 - 7 =$
$37 - 9 =$
$33 - 8 =$
$38 - 6 =$
$36 - 8 =$
$33 - 9 =$
$34 - 5 =$
$36 - 7 =$
$35 - 6 =$

B. Write the difference between each pair of numbers.

1.		**2.**		**3.**		**4.**	
90, 40		190, 60		300, 600		1800, 300	
30, 60		80, 150		500, 900		500, 1600	
40, 70		90, 130		700, 200		600, 1700	
90, 80		140, 60		500, 800		1200, 900	
60, 20		50, 170		600, 900		1500, 800	

Extension

C. Complete each of these.

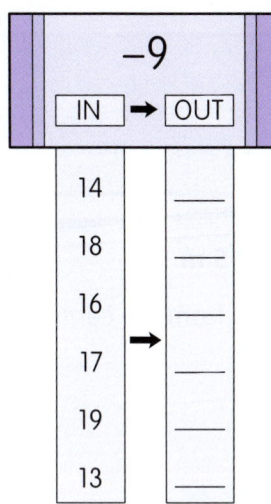
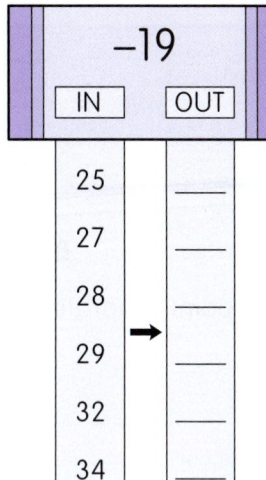

1.

−9

IN →	OUT
14	___
18	___
16	___
17	___
19	___
13	___

2.

−19

IN	OUT
25	___
27	___
28	___
29	___
32	___
34	___

3.

−29

IN	OUT
32	___
37	___
39	___
35	___
43	___
46	___

4.

−39

IN	OUT
45	___
48	___
44	___
46	___
54	___
51	___

D. Write the answers.

1. 15 subtract 7 ⟶ ☐

2. 80 take away 30 ⟶ ☐

3. 13 minus 8 ⟶ ☐

4. 50 minus 20 ⟶ ☐

5. 14 take away 6 ⟶ ☐

6. Reduce 90 by 20 ⟶ ☐

7. Decrease 12 by 4 ⟶ ☐

8. 70 subtract 30 ⟶ ☐

9. Reduce 16 by 9 ⟶ ☐

10. The difference between 600 and 200 ⟶ ☐

11. The difference between 8 and 19 ⟶ ☐

12. Decrease 900 by 400 ⟶ ☐

Challenge

E. Complete each number trail from 100 to zero.

1. (100) —−30→ (70) —−50→ ( ) —−14→ ( ) —−6→ (0)

2. (100) —−20→ ( ) —−70→ ( ) —−6→ ( ) —−4→ (0)

3. (100) —−25→ ( ) —−15→ ( ) —−45→ ( ) —−15→ (0)

4. (100) —−5→ ( ) —−55→ ( ) —−35→ ( ) —−5→ (0)

TOPIC 4: **Length**

Focus

Length is measured in **millimetres, centimetres, metres** and **kilometres**.

1 kilometre (km) = 1000 metres (m)

1 metre (m) = 100 centimetres (cm)

1 centimetre (cm) = 10 millimetres (mm)

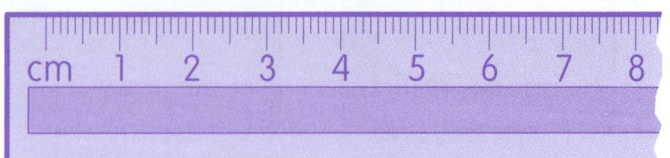

855 cm = 8.55 m

The point separates the metres from the centimetres.

Practice

A. Write these lengths.

1. 5000 m = _____ km

2. 10,000 m = _____ km

3. 3500 m = _____ km

4. 500 m = _____ km

5. 6 km = _____ m

6. 2000 cm = _____ m

7. 7.5 km = _____ m

8. 525 cm = _____ m

9. 200 cm = _____ m

10. 7 cm = _____ mm

11. 650 cm = _____ m

12. 6.35 m = _____ cm

13. 40 mm = _____ cm

14. 1.2 km = _____ m

15. 15 mm = _____ cm

16. 1745 cm = _____ m

B. Measure these lines with a ruler.

1. Measure these in centimetres.

_____ cm

_____ cm

_____ cm

_____ cm

2. Measure these in centimetres and write each length in millimetres.

_____ cm _____ mm

_____ cm _____ mm

_____ cm _____ mm

_____ cm _____ mm

Extension

C. Measure these and write the length of each in millimetres.

1. [____] mm

2. [____] mm

3. [____] mm

4. [____] mm

D. Write the answers.

1. A piece of ribbon is 45 cm long. 100 mm is cut off.
   How long is the piece of ribbon now? _____

2. A bus travels 4.5 km from Arnely to Boseworth.
   How far does it travel in total on a return journey? _____

3. What is 500 m less than 6 km? _____

4. Two shelves are 70 cm and 90 cm in length.
   What is their total length in metres and centimetres? _____

5. A tree is 3.5 metres tall. It doubles in height in a year.
   What is its height in centimetres after a year? _____

6. A family sets off to drive 480 km.
   After 250 km how much further have they to go? _____

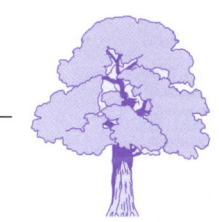

Challenge

E. Look at this ruler. What is the distance between the arrows?

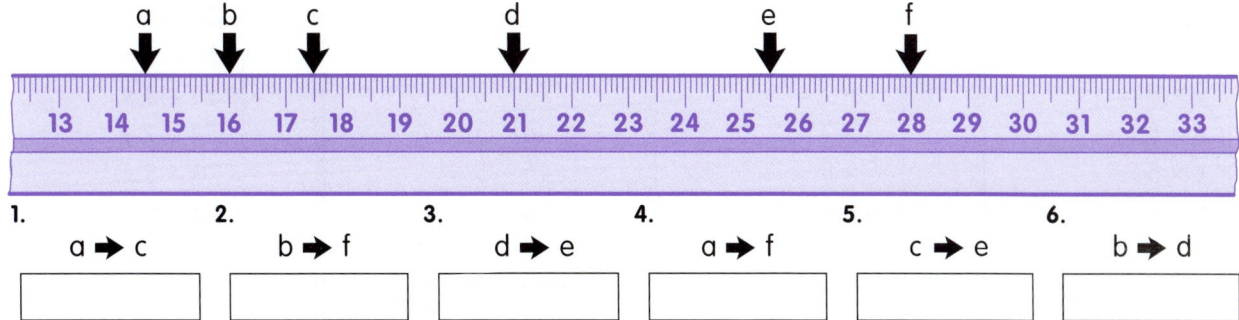

1. a ➡ c	2. b ➡ f	3. d ➡ e	4. a ➡ f	5. c ➡ e	6. b ➡ d
[____]	[____]	[____]	[____]	[____]	[____]

TOPIC 5: **Multiplication and division facts**

Focus

If you know your multiplication facts, it can help you learn the division facts.

For every fact, you can work out another three facts very easily. Look at this for the trio 4, 6 and 24:

$4 \times 6 = 24$

$6 \times 4 = 24$

$24 \div 4 = 6$

$24 \div 6 = 4$

Remember **6 x 4** and **4 x 6** give the same answer – it doesn't matter which way round you multiply.

Practice

A. Write the missing numbers for each trio.

1. **7, 5, 35** ___ × 7 = ___   ___ × ___ = 35   35 ÷ ___ = ___   ___ ÷ 7 = ___

2. **4, 9, 36** ___ × 4 = ___   ___ × ___ = 36   36 ÷ ___ = ___   ___ ÷ 4 = ___

3. **3, 6, 18** ___ × 3 = ___   ___ × ___ = 18   18 ÷ ___ = ___   ___ ÷ 3 = ___

4. **6, 5, 30** ___ × 6 = ___   ___ × ___ = 30   30 ÷ ___ = ___   ___ ÷ 6 = ___

5. **9, 3, 27** ___ × ___ = ___   ___ × ___ = ___   ___ ÷ ___ = ___   ___ ÷ ___ = ___

6. **7, 6, 42** ___ × ___ = ___   ___ × ___ = ___   ___ ÷ ___ = ___   ___ ÷ ___ = ___

7. **8, 9, 72** ___ × ___ = ___   ___ × ___ = ___   ___ ÷ ___ = ___   ___ ÷ ___ = ___

8. **6, 8, 48** ___ × ___ = ___   ___ × ___ = ___   ___ ÷ ___ = ___   ___ ÷ ___ = ___

B. Time how long it takes you to answer each block. Try to beat your best time.

1.	2.	3.	4.
$9 \times 5 =$	$3 \times 6 =$	$35 \div 5 =$	$36 \div 6 =$
$6 \times 4 =$	$6 \times 7 =$	$21 \div 7 =$	$32 \div 8 =$
$8 \times 8 =$	$5 \times 4 =$	$45 \div 9 =$	$28 \div 4 =$
$3 \times 9 =$	$4 \times 8 =$	$30 \div 6 =$	$36 \div 9 =$
$3 \times 8 =$	$7 \times 7 =$	$24 \div 8 =$	$21 \div 3 =$
$4 \times 6 =$	$3 \times 7 =$	$18 \div 3 =$	$14 \div 7 =$
$6 \times 5 =$	$5 \times 8 =$	$45 \div 5 =$	$20 \div 5 =$
$9 \times 9 =$	$6 \times 6 =$	$24 \div 4 =$	$24 \div 6 =$
$5 \times 9 =$	$8 \times 9 =$	$81 \div 9 =$	$54 \div 9 =$
$8 \times 6 =$	$4 \times 7 =$	$42 \div 7 =$	$56 \div 8 =$

Extension

C. Complete each table for these machines.

1.

IN	4			7		5	
OUT		18			54		48

2.
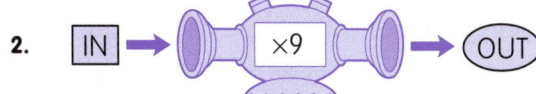

IN		6			7		4
OUT	45			18		81	

3.
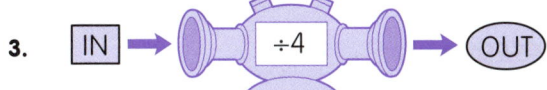

IN	28		36		16		
OUT		3		8			5

4.

IN		21		15			24
OUT	6		9		4		

Challenge

D. Complete these grids.

1.

×	6	8	4
3	18		
9			
2			

2.

×	4	9	3
8			
7			
5			

3.

×	4	6	7
2			
5			
8			

4.

×	4		8
	8	10	
3	12		24
6		30	

5.

×	3	7	
4		28	36
	21		63
	24	56	

6.

×		6	
	12	18	30
5	20		50
	40	60	100

TOPIC 6: **2D shapes**

Focus

A **polygon** is any 2D shape with straight sides. The sides and angles of a **regular polygon** are all equal. These are the names of some polygons.

Triangle	3 sides	
Quadrilateral	4 sides	
Pentagon	5 sides	
Hexagon	6 sides	

Heptagon	7 sides	
Octagon	8 sides	
Nonagon	9 sides	
Decagon	10 sides	

Some shapes have more than one name.

For example a **rectangle** is a quadrilateral with 4 right angles.

A **square** is a special rectangle because the four sides are equal.

Practice

A. Write one or more names for each shape. Tick the regular polygons.

1.

_____

2.

_____

3.

_____

4.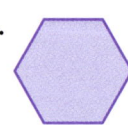

_____

5.

_____

6.

_____

7.

_____

8.

_____

9.

_____

10.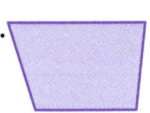

_____

11.

_____

12.

_____

13.

_____

14.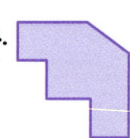

_____

15.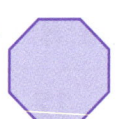

_____

Extension

B. Tick the odd one out in each set. Complete each sentence.

1. All _____ have 5 sides.

2. All _____ have 4 sides.

3. All _____ have 7 sides.

4. All _____ have 3 sides.

5. All _____ have 9 sides.

6. All _____ have 8 sides.

Challenge

C. Join each shape to the correct place on the Carroll diagram.

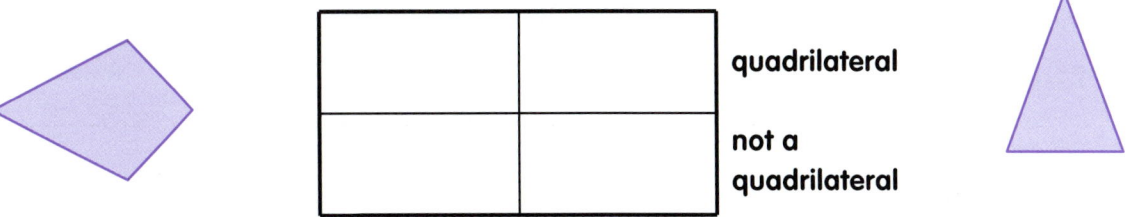

	right-angles	no right-angles
quadrilateral		
not a quadrilateral		

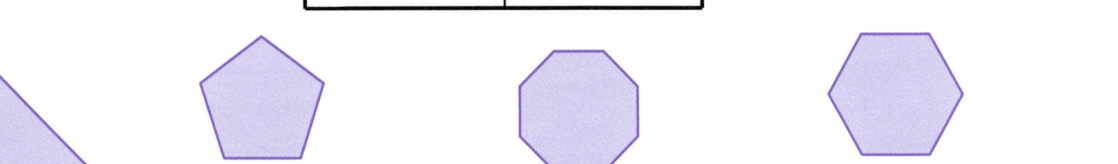

15

TEST 1 (Score 1 mark for every correct answer.)

Topic 1

1. Write this as a number:

   six thousand and forty-seven ☐

2. Write the missing numbers.

   7264 = ____ + ____ + 60 + 4

3. Write these in order starting with the smallest.

   6704   7064   6740   7604   6047

   _____   _____   _____   _____   _____

4. Write the value of the bold digit:

   62078 _____

Topic 2

5. Write the missing number.

   ☐ + 7 = 15

6. Write the total.

   40 + 80 = ☐

7. Complete these addition patterns:

   5 + 9 = ☐

   15 + 9 = ☐

   25 + 9 = ☐

8. What is the total of 5, 8 and 7?

   _____

Topic 3

9. Write the missing number.

   ☐ − 7 = 6

10. Write the difference between this pair of numbers.

    1500, 600 ➡ ☐

11. Write the number coming out of this machine.

    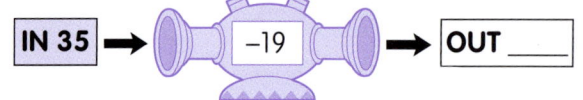

    IN 35 ➡ −19 ➡ OUT _____

12. What is 120 subtract 50?

    _____

Topic 4

13. Write the missing lengths.

80 mm = _____ cm   6500 m = _____ km

15. Write the length of this pencil. _____

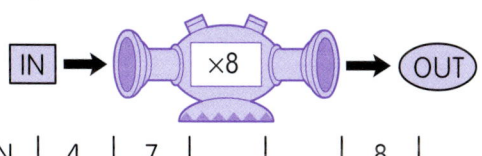

14. Write this length in centimetres and in millimetres.

 ___ cm ___ mm

16. What is the difference in length between two lines measuring 17 cm and 9 cm?

Topic 5

17. Write the missing numbers for this trio:

8, 4, 32   ___ × 4 = ___   ___ × ___ = 32   ___ ÷ 4 = ___   32 ÷ ___ = ___

18. Answer these.   7 × 6 = ☐   32 ÷ 4 = ☐

19. Complete the table for this machine.

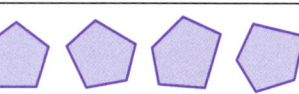

IN	4	7			8	
OUT			48	72		16

20. Complete this grid.

×	3	8	
4			
		48	
9			63

Topic 6

21. Name these shapes. _____

Tick the regular shape.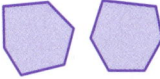

23. Tick the odd one out.

22. Write two names for this shape.

_____   _____

24. Tick the right angles.

Mark the test. Remember to fill in your score on page 3.

Write your score out of 24. ☐

Add a BONUS POINT if you scored 20 or more.

TOTAL SCORE FOR TEST 1 ☐

How did you find the test?

Colour a face

too hard   too easy   about right

TOPIC 7: **Time**

Focus

Mornings and afternoons are shown by **am** and **pm**.

24 hours = 1 day

60 minutes = 1 hour

60 seconds = 1 minute

Twenty-past seven in the morning ➔ **7.20 am**

Twenty-past seven in the evening ➔ **7.20 pm**

Practice

A. Write the time shown by each clock.

1.

2.

3.

4.

5.
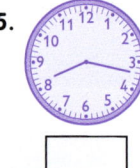

6.

7.
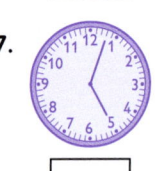

8.
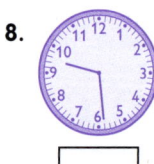

B. Draw hands to show these times.

1.

2.
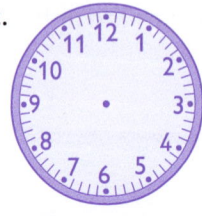

3.

4.
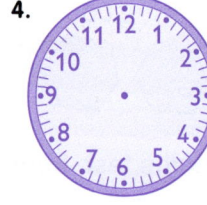

Extension

C. A coach takes 25 minutes between each stop. Complete the timetable.

Church Street	8.50 am	9.35 am	11.00 am	1.05 pm
Marsh Lane	9.15 am			
Hospital			11.50 am	
Swimming pool				2.20 pm

D. Answer these time problems.

1. A film started at the cinema at 6.35 pm. If it lasted for 90 minutes, what time did it finish?_____

2. Tom woke up at 7.30 am. If school begins at 8.55 am, how long has he got before it starts?_____

3. A football match lasts for 45 minutes each half, with a 15-minute break at half time. If the match starts at 11.30 am, what time will it finish? _____

4. A swimming session lasted 1 hour and 20 minutes. If it finished at 2.45 pm, when did the session start? _____

5. A car journey started at 9.45 am and finished at 3.50 pm. How long did the journey last? _____

Challenge

E. These clocks are all running slow. If the real time is 4.45, how many minutes slow is each clock?

1.
_____ minutes slow

2.
_____ minutes slow

3.
_____ minutes slow

4.
_____ minutes slow

5.
_____ minutes slow

6.
_____ minutes slow

TOPIC 8: **Fractions of shapes**

Focus

A fraction has two parts:

$$\frac{2}{3}$$ ←**numerator** (top number)
←**denominator** (bottom number)

1 part out of 3 shaded. This shows $\frac{1}{3}$.

2 parts out of 3 shaded. This shows $\frac{2}{3}$.

Fractions that have the same value are called **equivalent fractions**.

$\frac{1}{2}$ is the same as $\frac{2}{4}$

Practice

A. Write the fraction coloured on each of these.

1.

2.

3.

4.

5.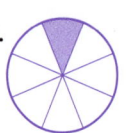

6.

7.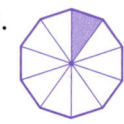

8.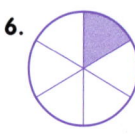

9.

10.

11.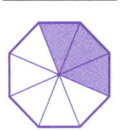

12.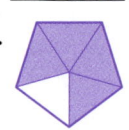

B. Write the equivalent fractions.

1. 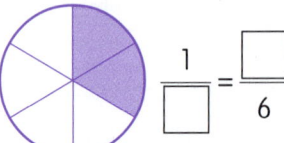 $\frac{1}{\Box} = \frac{\Box}{6}$

2. 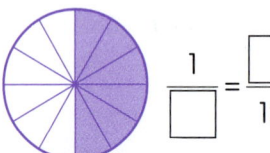 $\frac{1}{\Box} = \frac{\Box}{12}$

3. 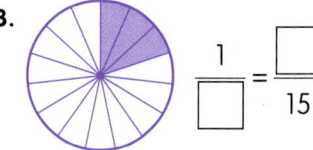 $\frac{1}{\Box} = \frac{\Box}{15}$

4. 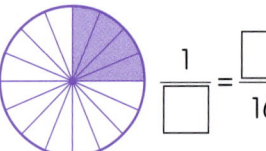 $\frac{1}{\Box} = \frac{\Box}{16}$

5. 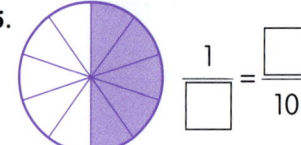 $\frac{1}{\Box} = \frac{\Box}{10}$

6. 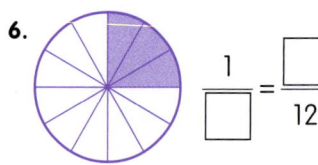 $\frac{1}{\Box} = \frac{\Box}{12}$

Extension

C. Write the fraction shaded.

1.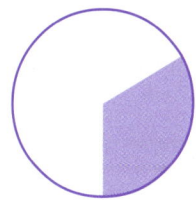

2.

3.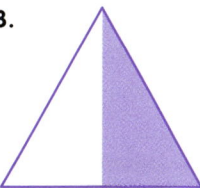

4.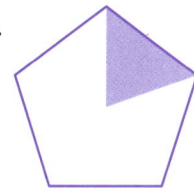

_____ _____ _____ _____

5.

6.

_____ _____

D. Shade these strips to show the fractions.

1. $\frac{3}{4}$ 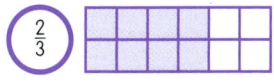 2. $\frac{2}{3}$ 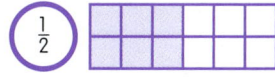 3. $\frac{1}{2}$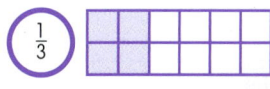

4. $\frac{2}{5}$ 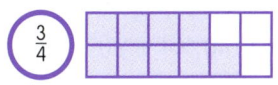 5. $\frac{1}{3}$ 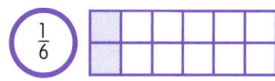 6. $\frac{1}{4}$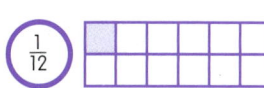

Challenge

E. Write these fractions in order, starting with the smallest.

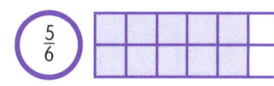

$\frac{2}{3}$ $\frac{1}{2}$ $\frac{1}{3}$ $\frac{1}{4}$

$\frac{3}{4}$ $\frac{1}{6}$ $\frac{5}{6}$ $\frac{1}{12}$

_____ _____ _____ _____ _____ _____ _____ _____

TOPIC 9: **Addition**

Focus

There are lots of different ways to add up numbers in your head.
One way is to break up numbers to make them easier to add.

For example:

46 + 37

Try using these three steps:

1. Hold the bigger number in your head: ∘∘∘ ⟨ 46 ⟩

2. Add the tens: ∘∘∘ ⟨ 46 + 30 = 76 ⟩

3. Add the units: ∘∘∘ ⟨ 76 + 7 = 83 ⟩

Practice

A. Look at these numbers. Work out the different totals.

60 → a   40 → b   80 → c   50 → d   35 → e   55 → f   25 → g   75 → h

1. a + d → ☐
2. a + g → ☐
3. e + g → ☐

4. b + c → ☐
5. e + c → ☐
6. f + e → ☐

7. c + d → ☐
8. h + d → ☐
9. h + g → ☐

10. b + a → ☐
11. g + c → ☐
12. f + h → ☐

B. Answer these mentally.

1. $45 + 50 =$ ☐   2. $60 + 55 =$ ☐   3. $80 + 43 =$ ☐   4. $28 + 70 =$ ☐   5. $90 + 67 =$ ☐

6. $42 + 34 =$ ☐   7. $23 + 65 =$ ☐   8. $43 + 36 =$ ☐   9. $57 + 33 =$ ☐   10. $61 + 28 =$ ☐

11. $58 + 34 =$ ☐   12. $57 + 25 =$ ☐   13. $63 + 28 =$ ☐   14. $42 + 49 =$ ☐   15. $54 + 27 =$ ☐

16. $74 + 52 =$ ☐   17. $62 + 85 =$ ☐   18. $55 + 76 =$ ☐   19. $83 + 58 =$ ☐   20. $74 + 68 =$ ☐

C. Add the rows. Add the columns. Add all four totals to make the corner number.

1.

53	47	
28	31	

2.

31	67	
42	39	

3.

62	57	
38	29	

4.

62	53	
74	47	

D. Join pairs which total 111.

74

68

67

47

78

57

44

37

64

54

33

43

E. Write the missing digits 3 to 8 to complete these.

1. $28 + \bigcirc 7 = 9\bigcirc$ 2. $59 + \bigcirc 4 = 1\bigcirc 3$ 3. $\bigcirc 1 + 6\bigcirc = 145$

23

TOPIC 10: **Subtraction**

Focus

There are lots of different ways to subtract numbers in your head.

One way is to find the difference by counting on from the smallest number.

This number line shows the method to work out **84 − 47**.

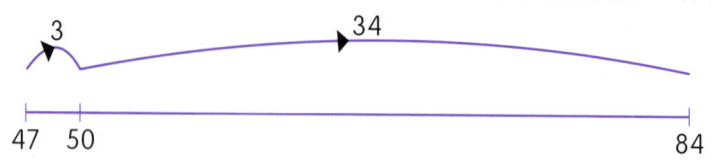

Count on from 47 to 50. Hold the 3 in your head.

50 to 84 is 34.

34 + 3 is 37.

So **84 − 47 = 37**

Practice

A. Draw the jumps on the number lines to help answer these.

1. 74 − 36 = ☐   36 ———————— 74

2. 83 − 46 = ☐   46 ———————— 83

3. 61 − 37 = ☐   37 ———————— 61

4. 73 − 49 = ☐   49 ———————— 73

5. 45 − 28 = ☐   28 ———————— 45

6. 85 − 57 = ☐   57 ———————— 85

7. 72 − 46 = ☐   46 ———————— 72

8. 67 − 38 = ☐   38 ———————— 67

9. 81 − 64 = ☐   64 ———————— 81

10. 92 − 57 = ☐   57 ———————— 92

B. Answer these mentally.

1. 58 − 37 = ☐   **2.** 74 − 41 = ☐   **3.** 85 − 63 = ☐   **4.** 76 − 32 = ☐   **5.** 87 − 53 = ☐

6. 52 − 18 = ☐   **7.** 43 − 16 = ☐   **8.** 61 − 14 = ☐   **9.** 57 − 19 = ☐   **10.** 72 − 17 = ☐

11. 64 − 28 = ☐   **12.** 42 − 25 = ☐   **13.** 53 − 28 = ☐   **14.** 56 − 29 = ☐   **15.** 65 − 27 = ☐

16. 94 − 57 = ☐   **17.** 72 − 45 = ☐   **18.** 85 − 46 = ☐   **19.** 93 − 68 = ☐   **20.** 84 − 58 = ☐

Extension

C. The number in the circle is the difference between the two numbers.

Write the missing numbers.

1. 36 ◄ ( ) ► 54   2. 29 ◄ ( ) ► 45   3. 62 ◄ ( ) ► 71   4. 51 ◄ ( ) ► 67

5. 28 ◄ ( ) ► 56   6. 67 ◄ ( ) ► 84   7. 45 ◄ ( ) ► 61   8. 67 ◄ ( ) ► 92

D. Join pairs with a difference of 44.

83   96   77
62
93   97
52   39
33   18
53   49

Challenge

E. Write the missing digits 3 to 8 to complete these.

1. $8\bigcirc - \bigcirc 7 = 26$ 2. $9\bigcirc - \bigcirc 8 = 26$ 3. $\bigcirc 4 - 4\bigcirc = 26$

TOPIC 11: Sequences and patterns

Focus

A number **sequence** is a list of numbers in a pattern. To find the rule or pattern in a sequence it can help to find the differences between each number.

$$1 \xrightarrow{+4} 5 \xrightarrow{+4} 9 \xrightarrow{+4} 13$$

The rule or pattern is **+4**

$$32 \xrightarrow{-3} 29 \xrightarrow{-3} 26 \xrightarrow{-3} 23$$

The rule or pattern is **−3**

Practice

A. Write the next three numbers in each sequence.

1.	2.	3.	4.	5.	6.	7.	8.	9.	10.
7	7	117	230	85	900	14	2	55	200
9	12	119	240	80	800	17	6	52	190
11	17	121	250	75	700	20	10	49	180
13	22	123	260	70	600	23	14	46	170

B. Write the missing three numbers in each sequence.

1.	2.	3.	4.	5.	6.	7.	8.	9.	10.
18			26	97	105		93		910
21	78		30	110		73		50	810
	73	510	34	115		64	85	53	
27	68	560		103		55	81	56	610
	63	610	42	105	130		77	59	
33		660		107		37			410

Extension

C. Write the four missing numbers in each sequence.

1. [ ] , [ ] , −3, −2, −1, 0, [ ] , [ ]
2. [ ] , [ ] , −15, −10, −5, 0, [ ] , [ ]
3. [ ] , [ ] , −4, −3, −2, −1, [ ] , [ ]
4. [ ] , [ ] , −12, −9, −6, −3, [ ] , [ ]
5. [ ] , [ ] , −10, −8, −6, −4, [ ] , [ ]
6. [ ] , [ ] , −4, −1, 2, 5, [ ] , [ ]
7. [ ] , [ ] , −7, −5, −3, −1, [ ] , [ ]
8. [ ] , [ ] , −10, −6, −2, 2, [ ] , [ ]

D. Two numbers in each sequence have been swapped over.

Circle the two numbers.

1. 28, 29, 35, 31, 32, 33, 34, 30
2. 15, 19, 23, 31, 27, 35, 39
3. 53, 51, 43, 47, 45, 49, 41
4. 480, 478, 468, 474, 472, 470, 476
5. 950, 910, 930, 920, 940, 900, 890
6. 150, 149, 144, 147, 146, 145, 148

Challenge

E. Follow the instructions for this number square. Look for any patterns.

- Colour the number 3.
- Count on 3 and colour 6.
- Keep counting on 3 and continue the pattern.
- Circle the number 2.
- Count on 2 and circle 4.
- Keep counting on 2 and continue the pattern.

1	2	3	4	5	6	7	8
9	10	11	12	13	14	15	16
17	18	19	20	21	22	23	24
25	26	27	28	29	30	31	32
33	34	35	36	37	38	39	40
41	42	43	44	45	46	47	48
49	50	51	52	53	54	55	56
57	58	59	60	61	62	63	64

TOPIC 12: Comparing and ordering numbers

Focus

When you need to put numbers in order it can help to write them under each other, lining up the units.

For example:

2370	387
387	438
1307	1307
438	2370

We use **<** and **>** to compare numbers.

< means **is less than**

For example: **475 < 580**

475 is less than 580

> means **is greater than**

For example: **764 > 746**

764 is greater than 746

Practice

A. Write these numbers in order, starting with the smallest.

1. 368, 860, 306, 380, 800, 806 _____ _____ _____ _____ _____ _____

2. 405, 590, 450, 594, 486, 589 _____ _____ _____ _____ _____ _____

3. 689, 966, 659, 965, 690, 906 _____ _____ _____ _____ _____ _____

4. 215, 512, 522, 205, 505, 520 _____ _____ _____ _____ _____ _____

5. 3125, 3502, 2599, 3005, 3152 _____ _____ _____ _____ _____

6. 1706, 1670, 7611, 7509, 5799 _____ _____ _____ _____ _____

7. 8345, 8543, 8095, 8307, 8079 _____ _____ _____ _____ _____

8. 7324, 7244, 7323, 7332, 7342 _____ _____ _____ _____ _____

B. Write the sign < or > for each pair of numbers.

1. 345 ☐ 428   2. 614 ☐ 641   3. 508 ☐ 505   4. 617 ☐ 609

5. 934 ☐ 919   6. 2453 ☐ 2540   7. 1800 ☐ 1798   8. 4976 ☐ 4967

9. 7806 ☐ 7860   10. 1799 ☐ 1800

Extension

C. Write the half-way number on each of these number lines.

1. 680 [ ] 690

2. 4000 [ ] 4100

3. 520 [ ] 540

4. 5640 [ ] 5740

5. 850 [ ] 870

6. 1010 [ ] 1110

7. 340 [ ] 440

8. 6450 [ ] 6500

9. 670 [ ] 770

10. 8320 [ ] 8360

D. Write the signs < or > for these.

1. 502 __ 567 __ 387

2. 7400 __ 7066 __ 7060

3. 2398 __ 2400 __ 2402

4. 399 __ 309 __ 394

5. 3654 __ 3746 __ 3577

6. 6983 __ 6098 __ 5277

Challenge

E. This table shows the area of some of the largest islands in Europe.
Write them in size order,
starting with the largest.

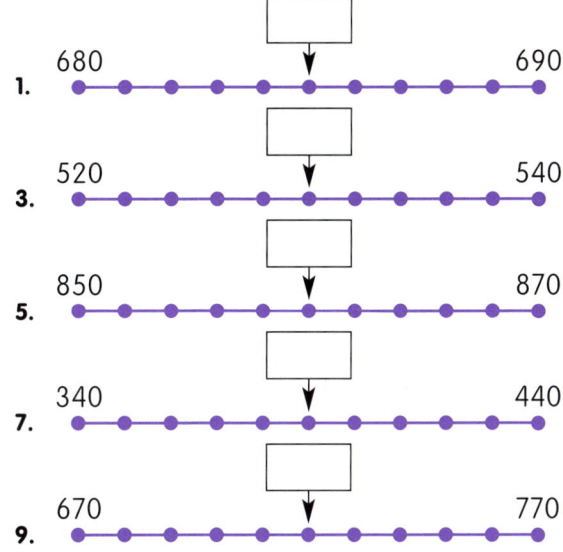
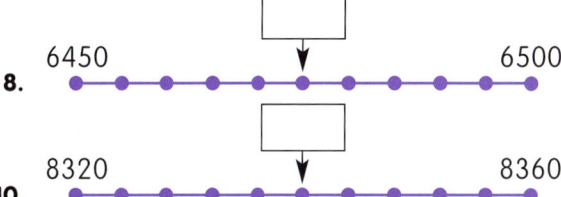

Island	Area (sq km)
Corsica	8270
Crete	8260
Cyprus	9251
Great Britain	218,041
Iceland	103,000
Ireland	83,766
Sardinia	23,800
Sicily	25,400

Island	Area (sq km)

TEST 2 (Score 1 mark for every correct answer.)

Topic 7

1. Write the time shown.

 [ ]

2. Draw hands to show this time.

3. A pizza is ordered at 7.25 pm. If it finally arrived at 8.15 pm, how long did it take for the pizza to be delivered? [ ]

4. A clock is 25 minutes slow. If it shows 8.35, what is the real time? [ ]

Topic 8

5. Write the fraction that is shaded.

 _____

6. Write the equivalent fractions.

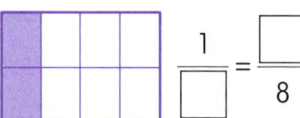 $\dfrac{1}{\Box} = \dfrac{\Box}{8}$

7. Write the fraction that is shaded.

 _____

8. Shade this strip to show the fraction $\frac{2}{3}$.

Topic 9

9. Write the total of these two numbers.

75 + 90 = [ ]

10. Answer this mentally.

65 + 87 = [ ]

11. Add the rows. Add the columns. Add all four totals to make the corner number.

53	47	
28	31	

12. Circle the two numbers that total 125.

67   59

76   58

79

30

Topic 10

13. Answer this.

85 – 47 = ☐

14. What is the difference between 73 and 45? ☐

15. Circle the two numbers that have a difference of 48.

83   87   45   38   93

16. Write the missing digits.

7☐ – ☐6 = 26

Topic 11

17. Write the next two numbers in this sequence.

8, 13, 18, 23, ☐, ☐

18. Write the missing numbers in this sequence.

70, 61, ☐, 43, ☐, 25

19. Write the four missing numbers.

☐, ☐, –8, –5, –2, 1, ☐, ☐

20. Two numbers have been swapped over. Circle the two numbers.

47, 45, 43, 37, 39, 41, 35

Topic 12

21. Write these numbers in order, starting with the smallest.

4769, 4799, 4679, 7649, 4767, 7697

_____ _____ _____ _____ _____ _____

22. Write the sign < or > for each pair of numbers.

6105 ___ 6150

4355 ___ 4335

23. Write the half-way number.

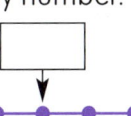

4120   4320

24. Write the sign < or > for these.

6104___3259___3260

Mark the test. Remember to fill in your score on page 3.

Write your score out of 24. ☐

Add a BONUS POINT if you scored 20 or more.

TOTAL SCORE FOR TEST 2 ☐

How did you find the test?

Colour a face

too hard   too easy   about right

TOPIC 13: **Rounding numbers**

Rounding makes numbers easier to work with – changing them to the nearest ten or hundred.

It is useful for estimating approximate answers.

Rounding to the nearest 10	**Rounding to the nearest 100**
Look at the **units** digit.	Look at the **tens** digits.
If it is 5 or more, round up the tens digit.	If it is 5 or more, round up the hundreds digit.
If it is less than 5, the tens digit stays the same.	If it is less than 5, the hundreds digit stays the same.
28<u>5</u> rounds up to 290	42<u>6</u>1 rounds up to 4300
51<u>4</u> rounds down to 510	61<u>4</u>7 rounds down to 6100

Practice

A. Round these to the nearest 10.

1. 456 ▶ ☐   2. 283 ▶ ☐   3. 149 ▶ ☐   4. 305 ▶ ☐

5. 644 ▶ ☐   6. 838 ▶ ☐   7. 1474 ▶ ☐   8. 9281 ▶ ☐

9. 6955 ▶ ☐   10. 3046 ▶ ☐   11. 7654 ▶ ☐   12. 9217 ▶ ☐

B. Round these to the nearest 100.

1. 673 ▶ ☐   2. 457 ▶ ☐   3. 145 ▶ ☐   4. 565 ▶ ☐

5. 816 ▶ ☐   6. 937 ▶ ☐   7. 4914 ▶ ☐   8. 7845 ▶ ☐

9. 7683 ▶ ☐   10. 4138 ▶ ☐   11. 3977 ▶ ☐   12. 2656 ▶ ☐

C. Round these to the nearest pound.

1. £1.46 ▶ ☐   2. £4.53 ▶ ☐   3. £2.09 ▶ ☐   4. £6.27 ▶ ☐

5. £4.63 ▶ ☐   6. £8.50 ▶ ☐   7. £13.08 ▶ ☐   8. £16.49 ▶ ☐

9. £22.62 ▶ ☐    10. £38.59 ▶ ☐   11. £41.80 ▶ ☐    12. £73.86 ▶ ☐

Extension

D. Estimate which tens number each arrow points to.

1.
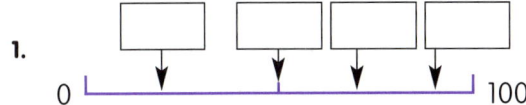
0   100

2.
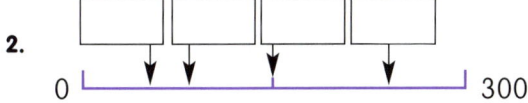
0   300

3.
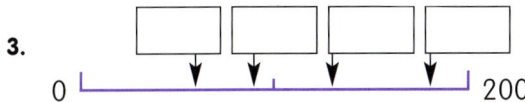
0   200

4.
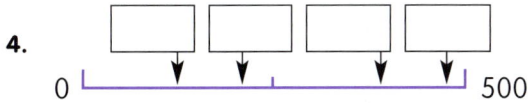
0   500

E. Estimate which hundreds number each arrow points to.

1.
0   1000

2.

0   3000

3.
0   2000

4.
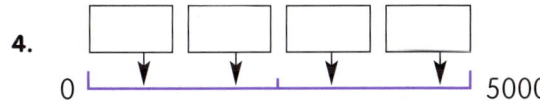
0   5000

Challenge

F. Estimate to give approximate answers.

1. Round these to the nearest 10.

149 + 232 ➡ ▭

308 + 434 ➡ ▭

593 – 418 ➡ ▭

746 – 338 ➡ ▭

33 × 19 ➡ ▭

47 × 22 ➡ ▭

2. Round these to the nearest 100.

4738 + 1229 ➡ ▭

6163 + 3442 ➡ ▭

4869 – 2345 ➡ ▭

7351 – 4138 ➡ ▭

221 × 381 ➡ ▭

542 × 386 ➡ ▭

33

TOPIC 14: **Weight and mass**

Focus

Weight and mass are closely linked but are not quite the same thing.

Mass is the amount of matter or material in an object.

Weight is the measurement of the force of gravity on an object.

Many books use the word 'weight' to mean the same as 'mass'.

Metric units of mass are **grams** and **kilograms**. There are 1000 grams in 1 kilogram.

$$1000 \text{ g} = 1 \text{ kg}$$
$$500 \text{ g} = \tfrac{1}{2} \text{ kg}$$

Practice

A. Write how many grams are in each of these measurements.

1. $2\frac{1}{2}$ kg = ☐ g
2. $3\frac{1}{4}$ kg = ☐ g
3. $\frac{3}{4}$ kg = ☐ g
4. $1\frac{1}{10}$ kg = ☐ g

5. 10.5 kg = ☐ g
6. $2\frac{3}{4}$ kg = ☐ g
7. 6.5 kg = ☐ g
8. $12\frac{3}{4}$ kg = ☐ g

B. Write these as kilograms and grams.

1. 2400 g = ☐ kg ☐ g
2. 1700 g = ☐ kg ☐ g
3. 3550 g = ☐ kg ☐ g
4. 5850 g = ☐ kg ☐ g

5. 1020 g = ☐ kg ☐ g
6. 4230 g = ☐ kg ☐ g
7. 6125 g = ☐ kg ☐ g
8. 1875 g = ☐ kg ☐ g

C. Write the weight of each parcel in kilograms and grams.

1.
2.
3.
4.
5.
6.

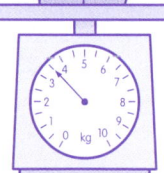 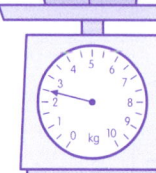 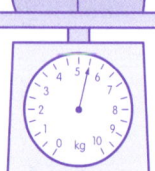 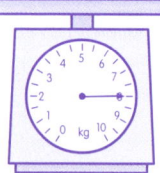 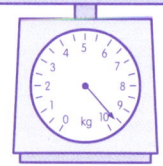 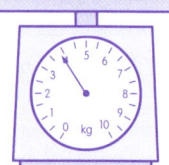

___ kg ___ g   ___ kg ___ g   ___ kg ___ g   ___ kg ___ g   ___ kg ___ g   ___ kg ___ g

Extension

D. Answer the problems.

 A 750 g

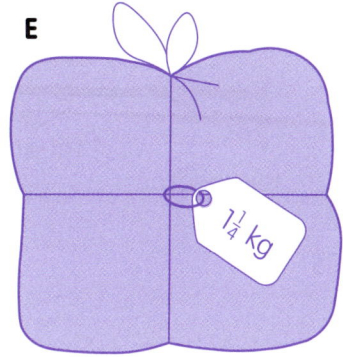 E 1¼ kg

 B 1 kg 200 g

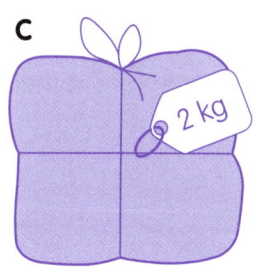 C 2 kg

 D 600 g

 F 900 g

1. What is the total weight of parcels A and E?

2. What is the difference in weight of parcels B and F?

3. Which parcel is 750 g lighter than parcel C?

4. How much heavier is parcel E than parcel B?

5. How much lighter is parcel B than parcel C?

6. Which two parcels have a total weight of 1½ kg?

Challenge

E. Round these to the nearest 100 g.

1.  4690 g [____] g

2.  5748 g [____] g

3. 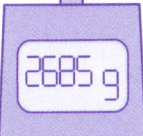 2685 g [____] g

4.  2067 g [____] g

5.  4505 g [____] g

6. 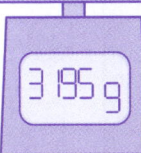 3185 g [____] g

35

TOPIC 15: **3D shapes**

Focus

3D means 3-dimensional and shows that it is a solid shape. Here are the names of some of these shapes.

  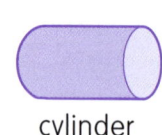 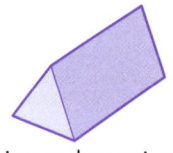 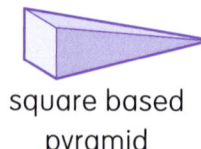 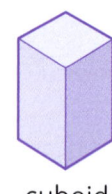

cube   hemisphere   cylinder   triangular prism   tetrahedron   square based pyramid   cuboid

We can talk about how many faces, corners (vertices) and edges a 3D shape has.

vertex

edge 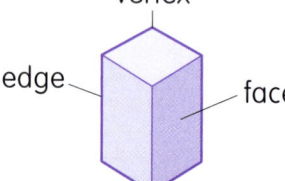 face

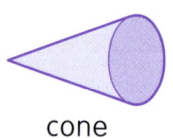 

cone   sphere

Practice

A. Name each of these shapes.

1.

_____

2.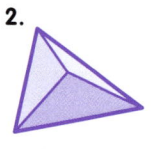

3.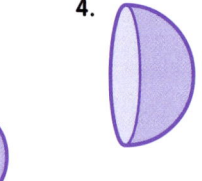

_____

4.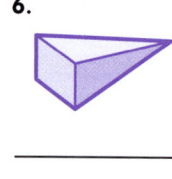

_____

5.

6.

7.

_____

B. Tick the odd shape out in each set.

1.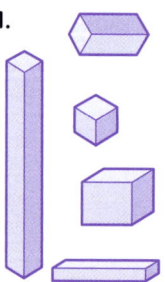

2.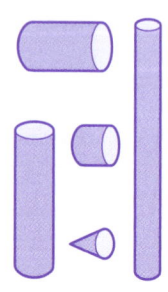

3.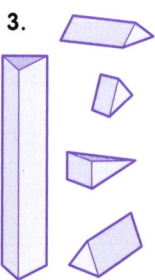

4.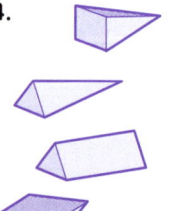

5.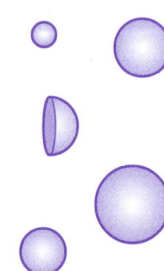

36

C. How many faces are there in each of these 3D shapes? Complete these sentences.

1.

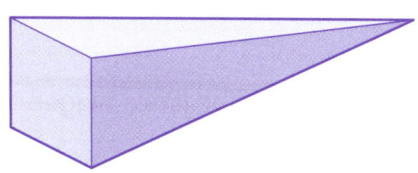

_____ square face and _____ triangular faces

2.

_____ triangular faces and _____ rectangular faces

3.

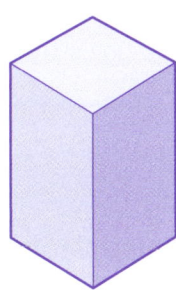

_____ square faces and _____ rectangular faces

4.

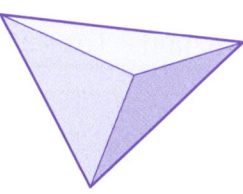

_____ triangular faces

Challenge

D. The name of each shape is muddled around. Try to work out each one from the clues.

1. Six square faces – the shape of a dice.

   BUCE _____

2. Four triangular faces – a special pyramid.

   TORNHEARTED _____

3. Two square faces and four rectangular faces – a good name for a box.

   CODUBI _____

4. A circular face and no point – half a marble.

   SHEPHERIME _____

TOPIC 16 : **Multiplication**

Focus

If you know your tables, it is easier to multiply bigger numbers in your head.

Example

To multiply tens by a single digit, work out the table fact and then make it ten times bigger:

$70 \times 5 = 7 \times 5 \times 10 = 35 \times 10 = 350$

To multiply a 2-digit number by a single digit, break the 2-digit number up.

38 × 4

1. Multiply the tens: $\quad 30 \times 4 = 120$
2. Multiply the units: $\quad 8 \times 4 = 32$
3. Add the two parts: $120 + 32 = 152$

Practice

A. Write the answers.

1. $20 \times 3 = \boxed{}$
2. $60 \times 2 = \boxed{}$
3. $40 \times 5 = \boxed{}$
4. $70 \times 3 = \boxed{}$
5. $30 \times 4 = \boxed{}$

6. $50 \times 5 = \boxed{}$
7. $90 \times 6 = \boxed{}$
8. $30 \times 9 = \boxed{}$
9. $80 \times 4 = \boxed{}$
10. $70 \times 2 = \boxed{}$

11. $30 \times 8 = \boxed{}$
12. $20 \times 7 = \boxed{}$
13. $80 \times 3 = \boxed{}$
14. $40 \times 9 = \boxed{}$
15. $60 \times 4 = \boxed{}$

B. Double each number.

1. 14 → double → $\bigcirc$
2. 17 → double → $\bigcirc$
3. 19 → double → $\bigcirc$
4. 23 → double → $\bigcirc$

5. 31 → double → $\bigcirc$
6. 28 → double → $\bigcirc$
7. 43 → double → $\bigcirc$
8. 47 → double → $\bigcirc$

9. 160 → double → $\bigcirc$
10. 250 → double → $\bigcirc$
11. 370 → double → $\bigcirc$
12. 490 → double → $\bigcirc$

C. Answer these. Use a mental method.

1. $45 \times 4 = \boxed{}$
2. $23 \times 3 = \boxed{}$
3. $37 \times 5 = \boxed{}$
4. $24 \times 3 = \boxed{}$
5. $42 \times 5 = \boxed{}$

6. $51 \times 3 = \boxed{}$
7. $63 \times 5 = \boxed{}$
8. $58 \times 2 = \boxed{}$
9. $64 \times 4 = \boxed{}$
10. $55 \times 3 = \boxed{}$

11. $69 \times 4 = \boxed{}$
12. $74 \times 5 = \boxed{}$
13. $86 \times 2 = \boxed{}$
14. $79 \times 3 = \boxed{}$
15. $88 \times 4 = \boxed{}$

Extension

D. Answer these problems.

1. What is 43 multiplied by 6? ☐

2. There are 24 hours in a day. How many hours are there in a week? ☐

3. Sam scored 49 points in a game. Jo scored double Sam's score. What did Jo score? ☐

4. Apples are packed with 64 to each box. How many apples are there in five boxes? ☐

5. A train ticket costs £38. What is the total cost for four tickets? ☐

6. What number is double 99? ☐

E. Use the grids to answer these.

1. 36×8

x	30	6
8	240	48

= 288

2. 53×7

x	50	3
7		

= ____

3. 46×9

x	40	6
9		

= ____

4. 78×6

x	70	8
6		

= ____

5. 68×7

x	60	8
7		

= ____

6. 79×8

x	70	9
8		

= ____

Challenge

F. Write the missing digits 1 to 6 to complete these.

1. $2\bigcirc \times 6 = \bigcirc 38$ 2. $\bigcirc 5 \times 7 = 31\bigcirc$ 3. $\bigcirc 8 \times 9 = 61\bigcirc$

TOPIC 17: **Division**

Focus

Division is the inverse or opposite of multiplication.
So if you know your tables, it will help you to divide numbers.

$$7 \times 3 = 21$$
$$21 \div 3 = 7$$
$$21 \div 7 = 3$$

There are several ways of writing a division:

$$30 \div 6$$
$$\frac{30}{6}$$
$$6\overline{)30}$$

All these mean 30 divided by 6.

Sometimes divisions aren't exact and leave **remainders**.

$$20 \div 3 = 6 \text{ remainder } 2 \quad \text{or} \quad 6r2$$

Practice

A. Write the answers.

1. $24 \div 3 = $ ☐   **2.** $18 \div 2 = $ ☐   **3.** $45 \div 5 = $ ☐   **4.** $30 \div 3 = $ ☐   **5.** $28 \div 4 = $ ☐

6. $60 \div 5 = $ ☐   **7.** $42 \div 6 = $ ☐   **8.** $32 \div 2 = $ ☐   **9.** $60 \div 4 = $ ☐   **10.** $54 \div 3 = $ ☐

11. $72 \div 3 = $ ☐   **12.** $76 \div 4 = $ ☐   **13.** $85 \div 5 = $ ☐   **14.** $78 \div 6 = $ ☐   **15.** $92 \div 4 = $ ☐

B. Halve each number.

1. 34 → ☐   **2.** 42 → ☐   **3.** 38 → ☐   **4.** 46 → ☐

5. 32 → ☐   **6.** 48 → ☐   **7.** 56 → ☐   **8.** 64 → ☐

9. 82 → ☐   **10.** 76 → ☐   **11.** 94 → ☐   **12.** 78 → ☐

C. Answer these. Remember to include the remainder.

1. $35 \div 4 = $ ☐ r ☐   **2.** $26 \div 3 = $ ☐ r ☐   **3.** $47 \div 2 = $ ☐ r ☐   **4.** $44 \div 3 = $ ☐ r ☐   **5.** $52 \div 5 = $ ☐ r ☐

6. $\frac{71}{3} = $ ☐ r ☐   **7.** $\frac{83}{2} = $ ☐ r ☐   **8.** $\frac{59}{4} = $ ☐ r ☐   **9.** $\frac{74}{5} = $ ☐ r ☐   **10.** $\frac{85}{3} = $ ☐ r ☐

11. $89 \div 6 = $ ☐ r ☐   **12.** $74 \div 8 = $ ☐ r ☐   **13.** $96 \div 9 = $ ☐ r ☐   **14.** $94 \div 7 = $ 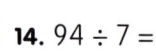 r    **15.** $98 \div 6 = $ 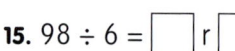 r ☐

Extension

D. Answer these problems.

1. What is 75 divided by 5? ☐

2. What number is half of 98? ☐

3. There are 54 children on a Cub outing. How many groups of six children can be made? ☐

4. Toby spent 84p on 6 pencils. How much was each pencil? ☐

5. I have 42 cakes. Each box holds 4 cakes. How many boxes will I need? ☐

6. A magazine costs £3 each month. Jack has £38. How many magazines will he be able to get? ☐

E. Match each division to a remainder. Write a division for the spare remainder.

| 56 ÷ 6 | | 71 ÷ 8 | | 96 ÷ 5 | | 86 ÷ 8 |

Remainder

1
2
3
4
5
6
7
8
9

÷

| 77 ÷ 9 | | 99 ÷ 10 | | 89 ÷ 9 | | 52 ÷ 7 |

Challenge

F. Write the missing digits 1 to 6 to complete these.

1. $75 \div \bigcirc = 2\bigcirc$ 2. $9\bigcirc \div 2 = \bigcirc 6$ 3. $\bigcirc 2 \div 2 = \bigcirc$

41

TOPIC 18: **Coordinates**

Coordinates show the exact position of a point on a grid.

The coordinates of A are (2,4)

The coordinates of B are (4,2)

Read the **horizontal** coordinate first and then the **vertical** coordinate.

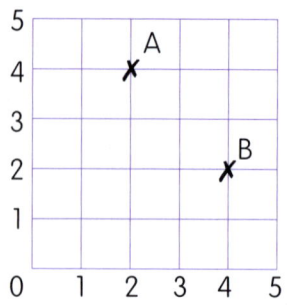

Practice

A. Look at these points and answer the questions.

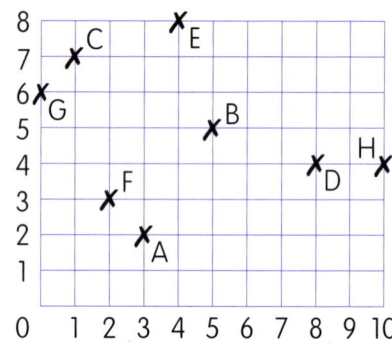

Write the coordinates of these:

A → (____,____)   F → (____,____)

D → (____,____)   H → (____,____)

Write the letters for each of these positions:

(5,5) ⬚   (0,6) ⬚   (4,8) ⬚   (1,7) ⬚

B. Plot and label these coordinates on the grid.

A = (4,1)   **B** = (6,2)   **C** = (0,1)   **D** = (5,4)   **E** = (2,0)   **F** = (8,7)   **G** = (9,3)   **H** = (7, 5)

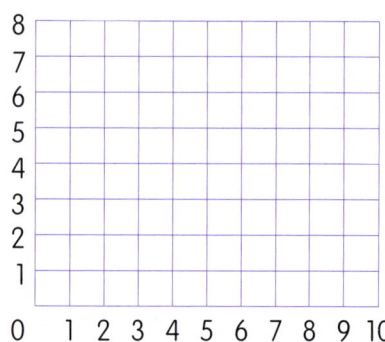

42

Extension

C. Plot these coordinates on the grid.

Use a ruler to join up the points in order to draw a shape.

A = (3,4)   B = (4,6)   C = (5,4)   D = (7,3)

E = (5,2)   F = (4,0)   G = (3,2)   H = (1,3)

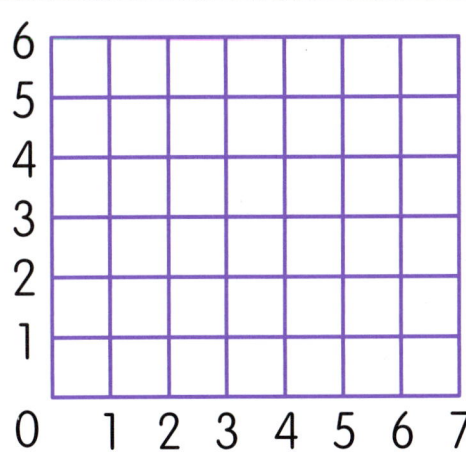

D. Design your own star on this grid.

Write the coordinates to show the position of each point.

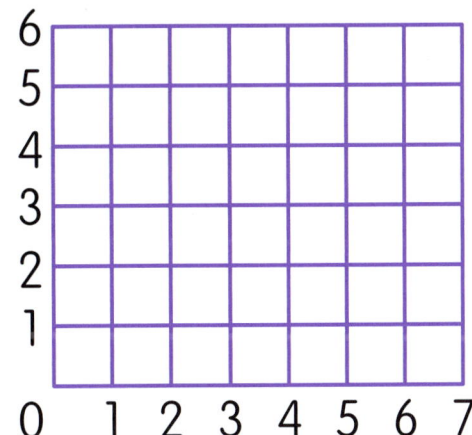

Challenge

E. Here are three corners of a rectangle.

1. What are the coordinates of the three corners?

   A → (____,____)   **B** → (____,____)   **C** → (____,____)

2. What would be the coordinates of the fourth corner, **D**? ☐

3. Plot the coordinate and complete the rectangle.

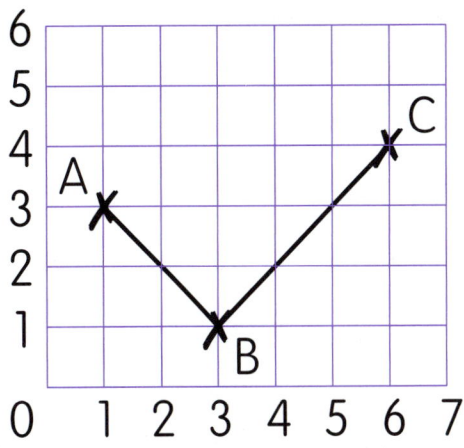

43

TEST 3 (Score 1 mark for every correct answer.)

Topic 13

1. Round these to the nearest 10.

543 ➤ ☐

6446 ➤ ☐

2. Round these to the nearest 100.

752 ➤ ☐

3148 ➤ ☐

3. Round these to the nearest pound.

£3.62 ➤ ☐

£24.50 ➤ ☐

4. Estimate which tens number each arrow points to.

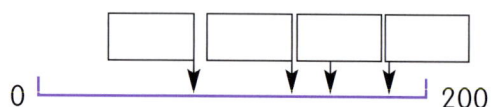

0 ———————— 200

Topic 14

5. Write the missing amount.

$8\frac{1}{10}$ kg = ☐ g

6. Write this as kilograms and grams.

6225 g = ☐ kg ☐ g

7. What is the weight of this parcel?

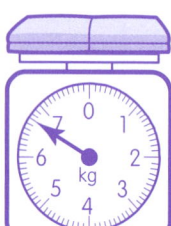

___ kg ___ g

8. What is the total weight of these two parcels?

250 g $2\frac{3}{4}$ kg

___ kg ___ g

Topic 15

9. Name this shape.

_____

10. Tick the odd shape out.

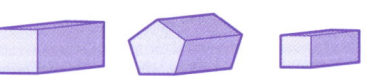

11. Count the faces of this shape and complete the sentence.

___ hexagon faces and ____ rectangular faces.

12. Which shape has a square face and four triangular faces?

_____

44

Topic 16

13. Write the answer.

$70 \times 4 =$ ☐

14. What is double 56? ☐

15. Answer this mentally.

$83 \times 3 =$ ☐

16. Bulbs are packed in boxes of six. How many bulbs are there in 25 boxes? ☐

Topic 17

17. Write the answer.

$64 \div 4 =$ ☐

18. What is half of 76? ☐

19. Answer this.

$4\overline{)78} =$ ☐ r ☐

20. Callum has 81p. He buys five ice lollies and gets 1p change. How much does each ice lolly cost? ☐

Topic 18

Look at these points and answer the questions.

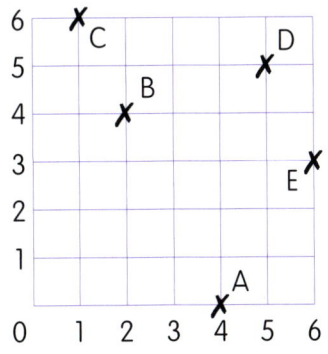

21. Write the coordinates for A (___ , ___)

22. Write the letter at position (1,6) ☐

23. Write the coordinates for E (___ , ___)

24. Draw a cross at position (3,5).

Mark the test. Remember to fill in your score on page 3.

Write your score out of 24.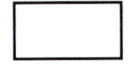

Add a BONUS POINT if you scored 20 or more.

TOTAL SCORE FOR TEST 3 ☐

How did you find the test?

Colour a face

too hard   too easy   about right

45

TOPIC 19: **Decimals**

A decimal point is used to separate whole numbers from fractions.

27.43

tens   units   tenths   hundredths

$\frac{1}{10} = 0.1$ $\frac{1}{2} = 0.5$

$\frac{2}{10} = 0.2$ $\frac{1}{100} = 0.01$

Practice

A. Write these as decimals.

1. $\frac{3}{10}$ →

2. $\frac{9}{10}$ →

3. $\frac{7}{10}$ →

4. $\frac{1}{2}$ →

5. $\frac{4}{10}$ →

6. $\frac{8}{10}$ →

7. $4\frac{1}{2}$ →

8. $2\frac{1}{10}$ →

9. $3\frac{7}{10}$ →

10. $5\frac{3}{10}$ →

11. $6\frac{9}{10}$ →

12. $4\frac{2}{10}$ →

B. Write the decimals on these lines.

1.
0 ——————————————————————— 1

2.
0 ——————————————————————— 1

3.
1 ——————————————————————— 2

4.
2 ——————————————————————— 3

5.
3 ——————————————————————— 4

6.
0 ——————————— 1 ——————————— 2

46

Extension

C. Write the value of the bold digit as a fraction.

1. 0.3**5** [ ]   **2.** 6.**8** [ ]   **3.** 14.7**5** [ ]   **4.** 0.0**2** [ ]   **5.** 9.**3**6 [ ]

6. 8.0**7** [ ]   **7.** 15.**6**9 [ ]   **8.** 4.1**5** [ ]   **9.** 10.**8** [ ]   **10.** 16.**4**7 [ ]

D. Put in the signs < or > so that these are true.

1. 4.65 kg [ ] 4.70 kg   **2.** 5.80 m [ ] 5.18 m   **3.** £3.65 [ ] £3.56   **4.** 3.25 [ ] 3.2

5. 3.15 [ ] 3.5   **6.** 6.05 [ ] 6.5   **7.** 2.34 [ ] 2.43   **8.** 8.66 [ ] 8.07

Challenge

E. Write these numbers in order, starting with the smallest.

1. 3.8   3.6   2.9   4   3   3.1   0.9

____ ____ ____ ____ ____ ____ ____

2. 4.8   8.32   0.8   8.3   0.4   4   8.1

____ ____ ____ ____ ____ ____ ____

3. 2.71   7.17   2   2.1   7.6   2.93   2.6

____ ____ ____ ____ ____ ____ ____

4. 10.35   10.14   10.4   3.06   11.1   10   3

____ ____ ____ ____ ____ ____ ____

TOPIC 20: **Capacity**

Focus

Capacity is all about how much something holds.
Metric units of capacity are litres and millilitres.

ml is short for millilitre.

l is short for litre.

There are **1000 millilitres** in **1 litre**.

$$1000\ ml = 1\ l$$
$$500\ ml = \tfrac{1}{2}\ l$$
$$100\ ml = \tfrac{1}{10}\ l$$

Practice

A. Write how many millilitres are in each of these measurements.

1. $1\tfrac{1}{2}\ l =$ [   ] ml   2. $2\tfrac{1}{4}\ l =$ [   ] ml   3. $\tfrac{1}{4}\ l =$ [   ] ml   4. $2\tfrac{1}{10}\ l =$ [   ] ml

5. $6.5\ l =$ [   ] ml   6. $4\tfrac{3}{4}\ l =$ [   ] ml   7. $8.5\ l =$ [   ] ml   8. $12\tfrac{3}{10}\ l =$ [   ] ml

B. Write these as litres and millilitres.

1. 4300 ml = ___ l ___ ml   2. 1900 ml = ___ l ___ ml   3. 6550 ml = ___ l ___ ml   4. 2350 ml = ___ l ___ ml

5. 2020 ml = ___ l ___ ml   6. 6730 ml = ___ l ___ ml   7. 4525 ml = ___ l ___ ml   8. 1975 ml = ___ l ___ ml

C. Write the amount shown in each jug.

1. 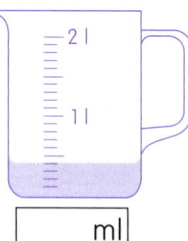 [   ] ml   2.  [   ] ml   3.  [   ] ml   4. 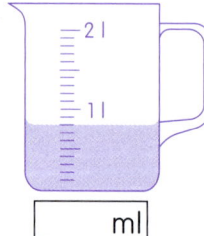 [   ] ml   5. [   ] ml

6.  [   ] ml   7.  [   ] ml   8. 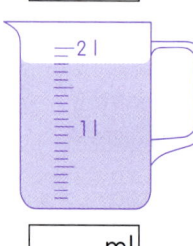 [   ] ml   9. 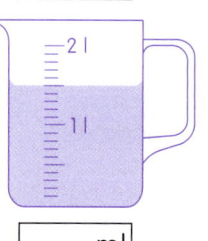 [   ] ml   10.  [   ] ml

Extension

D. Answer the problems.

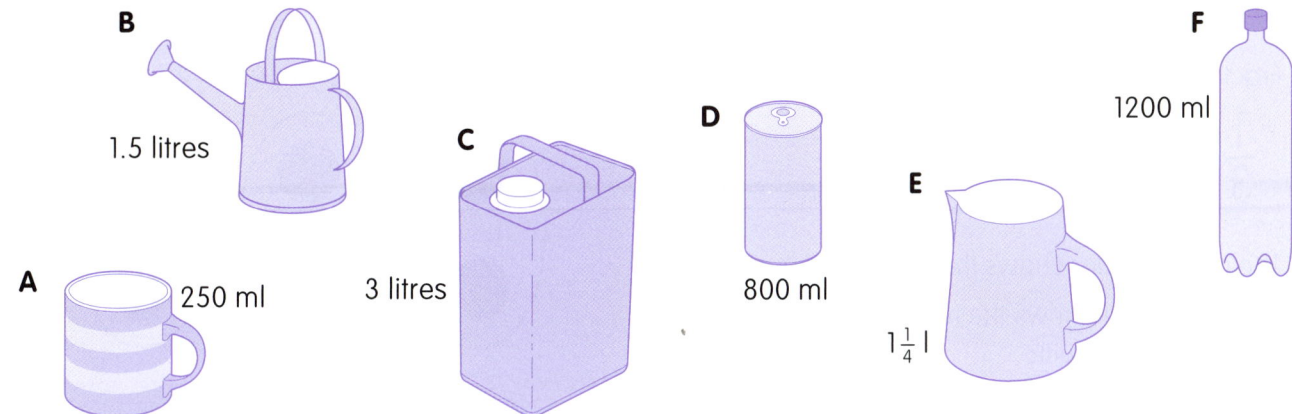

B
1.5 litres

C
3 litres

D
800 ml

E
$1\frac{1}{4}$ l

F
1200 ml

A
250 ml

1. What is the total capacity of containers A and E?

2. What is the difference in capacity of containers F and D?

3. Which container has double the capacity of container B?

4. How much more does container E hold than container F?

5. How much less does container A hold than container D?

6. Which two containers have a total capacity of 2 litres?

Challenge

E. Round these to the nearest 100 ml.

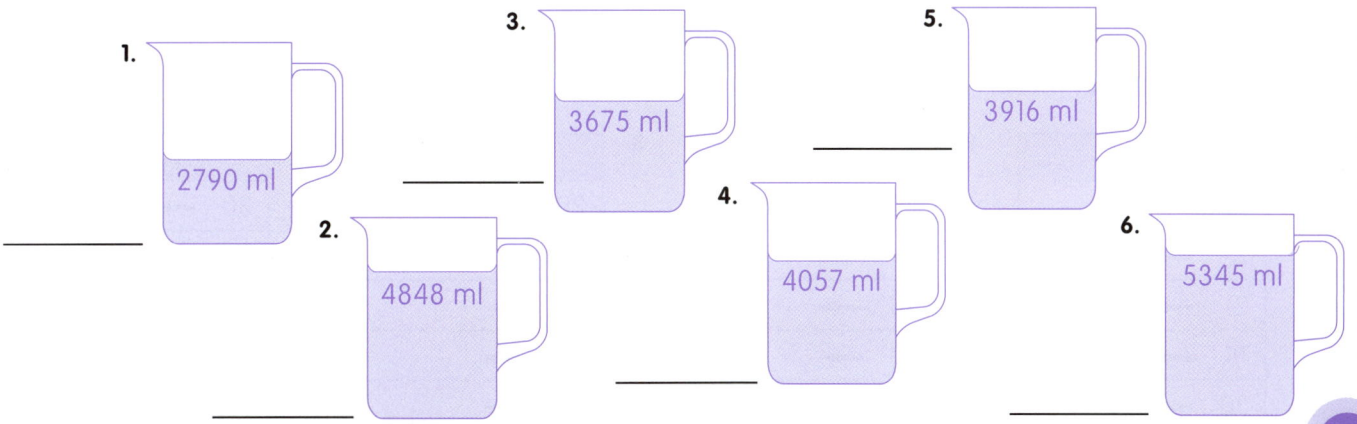

1. 2790 ml _____

2. 4848 ml _____

3. 3675 ml _____

4. 4057 ml _____

5. 3916 ml _____

6. 5345 ml _____

TOPIC 21: Fractions of amounts

Focus

Fractions have a **numerator** and a **denominator**.

$\dfrac{1}{3}$ ← **numerator** (top number)
$\dfrac{}{3}$ ← **denominator** (bottom number)

The denominator shows the number of equal parts.

The numerator shows the number of those parts you are dealing with.

$\frac{1}{3}$ of 6 is the same as $6 \div 3 = 2$

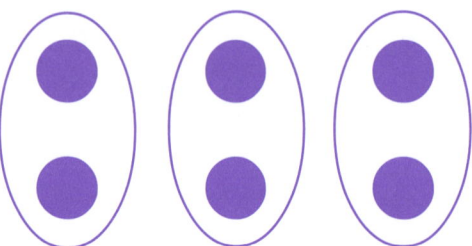

Practice

A. Work out the fraction of each amount.

1. Colour $\frac{1}{2}$ of the circles and write the answer.

○ ○ ○ ○ ○ ○ $\frac{1}{2}$ of 6 = ☐

○ ○ ○ ○ ○ ○ ○ ○ ○ ○ $\frac{1}{2}$ of 10 = ☐

○ ○ ○ ○ ○ ○ ○ ○ $\frac{1}{2}$ of 8 = ☐

○ ○ ○ ○ ○ ○ ○ ○ ○ ○ ○ ○ $\frac{1}{2}$ of 12 = ☐

2. Colour $\frac{1}{4}$ of the circles and write the answer.

○ ○ ○ ○ ○ ○ ○ ○ $\frac{1}{4}$ of 8 = ☐

○ ○ ○ ○ ○ ○ ○ ○ ○ ○ ○ ○ ○ ○ ○ ○ $\frac{1}{4}$ of 16 = ☐

○ ○ ○ ○ $\frac{1}{4}$ of 4 = ☐

○ ○ ○ ○ ○ ○ ○ ○ ○ ○ ○ ○ $\frac{1}{4}$ of 12 = ☐

B. Answer each of these.

1.

$\frac{1}{3}$ of …	
15	➡
12	➡
21	➡
18	➡
30	➡

2.

$\frac{1}{5}$ of …	
20	➡
15	➡
30	➡
40	➡
25	➡

3.

$\frac{1}{4}$ of …	
20	➡
32	➡
24	➡
40	➡
36	➡

4.

$\frac{1}{10}$ of …	
30	➡
80	➡
70	➡
60	➡
100	➡

Extension

C. Answer these.

1.
What fraction of £1 is:
50p →
20p →
10p →
25p →
75p →

2.
What fraction of £2 is:
20p →
£1 →
50p →
£1.50 →
40p →

3.
What fraction of £10 is:
£2.50 →
£5 →
£1 →
£7.50 →
£2 →

D. Answer these.

1.
What fraction of 1 kilogram is:
100 g →
400 g →
200 g →
500 g →
300 g →

2.
What fraction of 1 litre is:
250 ml →
750 ml →
600 ml →
800 ml →
700 ml →

3.
What fraction of 1 metre is:
50 cm →
25 cm →
10 cm →
75 cm →
20 cm →

Challenge

**E. Colour this grid to make a pattern.
Use these fractions for each colour.**

$\frac{1}{4}$ red

$\frac{1}{6}$ blue

$\frac{1}{12}$ yellow

$\frac{1}{3}$ green

$\frac{1}{8}$ orange

How many triangles are left white? [ ]

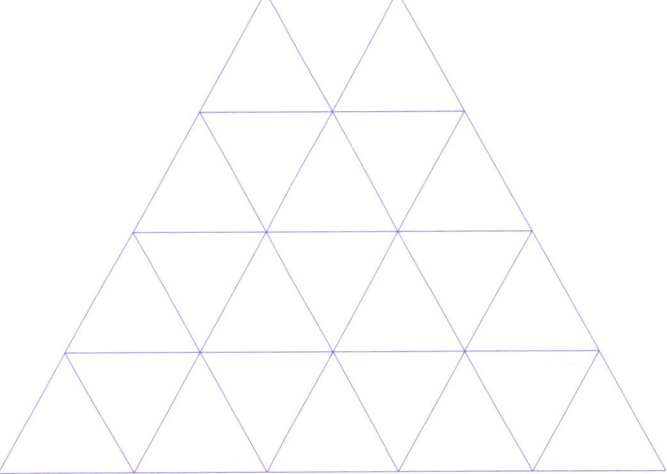

TOPIC 22: **Graphs**

Pictograms are graphs that have pictures.

Each picture stands for a number. Look at the **key** to see how many each picture stands for.

Some graphs have **bars** or **columns**.

The axes have **labels** that give you information.

You must look carefully at the numbered axis to see what **scale** is being used.

The scale does not always go up in ones.

Practice

Key

🔔 represents 5 visitors

🔔 represents between 0 and 5 visitors

A. This pictogram shows the number of visitors to a museum in a week.

Mon 🔔🔔🔔🔔🔔🔔🔔

Tues 🔔🔔🔔🔔🔔🔔🔔🔔

Wed

Thurs 🔔🔔🔔🔔

Fri 🔔🔔🔔🔔🔔🔔🔔

Sat 🔔🔔🔔🔔🔔🔔🔔🔔🔔

Sun 🔔🔔🔔🔔🔔🔔🔔

(axis label: Days)

Look at the pictogram and answer these questions.

1. How many visitors went to the museum on Tuesday? ☐

2. On which day did 37 people visit the museum? ☐

3. On which two days did the same number of people visit the museum? ☐

4. Approximately how many people visited the museum on Thursday? ☐

5. On which two days were there fewer visitors than on Monday? ☐

6. 14 of the visitors on Tuesday were children. How many adults were there on Tuesday? ☐

7. 88 people visited the museum at the weekend. How many visited on Saturday? ☐

8. Why do you think there were no visitors on Wednesday? ☐

B. This bar chart shows the results of a survey of the types of transport used by different visitors to get to the museum.

1. How many people came by train to the museum? ☐

2. How many fewer people cycled than came by bus? ☐

3. Which type of transport was used by 38 people? ☐

4. How many more people came by car than walked to the museum? ☐

5. How many people in total came by bus or by train? ☐

6. How many people were in the survey altogether? ☐

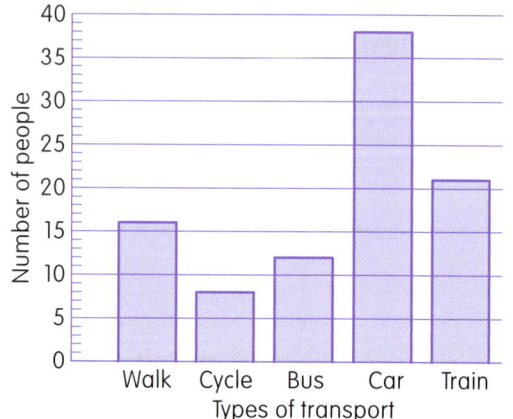

Extension

C. This bar chart shows the number of bikes sold each month by a bike shop.

Use the graph to answer these questions.

1. How many bikes were sold in June? ☐

2. In which month were the most bikes sold? ☐

3. In which month were 56 bikes sold? ☐

4. How many bikes were sold in total in July and August? ☐

5. In which month were half the number of bikes sold compared to December? ☐

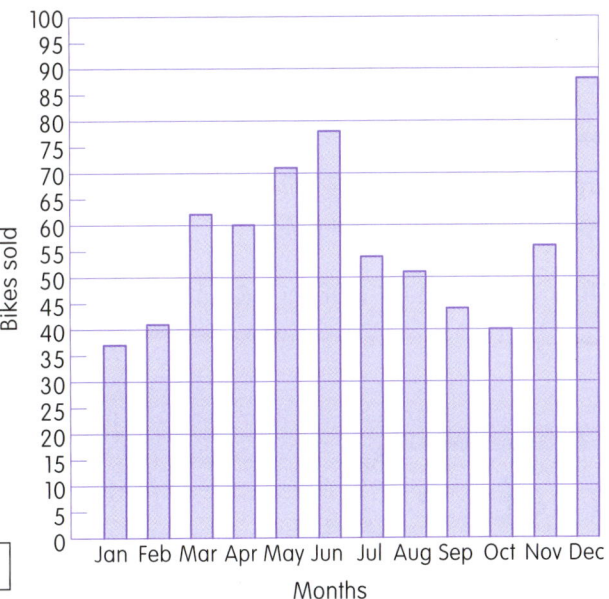

Challenge

D. This table of results shows the times of six riders in a cycle race.

Complete the graph and answer the questions.

Alan	Ben	Chris	David	Eric	Fred
48 mins	52 mins	39 mins	46 mins	43 mins	40 mins

1. Who had the fastest time? ☐

2. Which cyclist finished six minutes behind Fred? ☐

3. Which cyclist finished nine minutes ahead of Ben? ☐

4. Write the cyclists in the order they finished.

   _____   _____

   _____   _____

   _____   _____

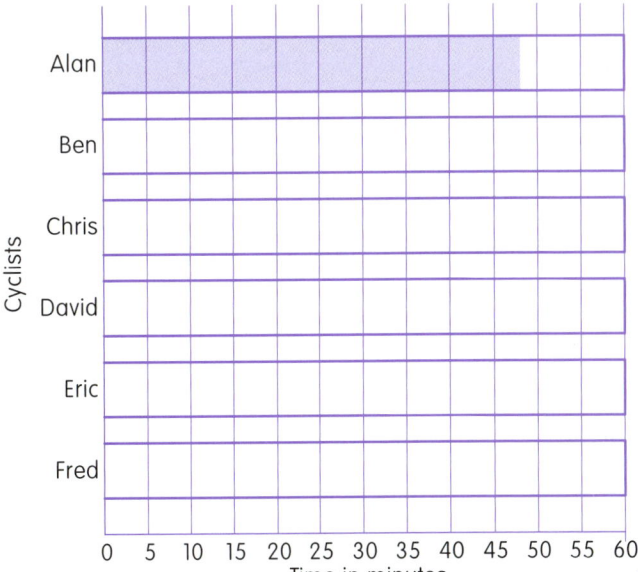

TOPIC 23: **Money**

Focus

There are 100 pence in £1. When we write amounts as pounds and pence, we separate the pounds from the pence with a decimal point.

£1.40 = 140p   £3.09 = 309p   £5.38 = 538p   £0.85 = 85p

Practice

A. Write these totals.

1.  ____ p
2. 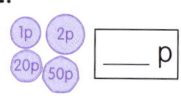 ____ p
3. 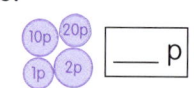 ____ p
4. ____ p

5. 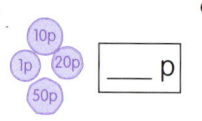 ____ p
6. 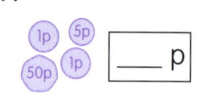 ____ p
7. 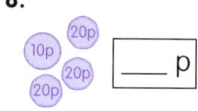 ____ p
8. 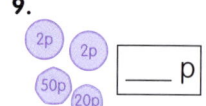 ____ p
9. 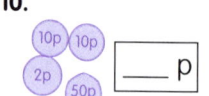 ____ p
10. ____ p

B. Write these amounts in a different way.

1. £1.25 → _____ p
2. £3.49 → _____ p
3. £2.08 → _____ p
4. £14.99 → _____ p

5. £12.81 → _____ p
6. £23.06 → _____ p
7. 149p → £_____
8. 227p → £_____

9. 503p → £_____
10. 1231p → £_____
11. 1466p → £_____
12. 69p → £_____

C. Write the change from each of these.

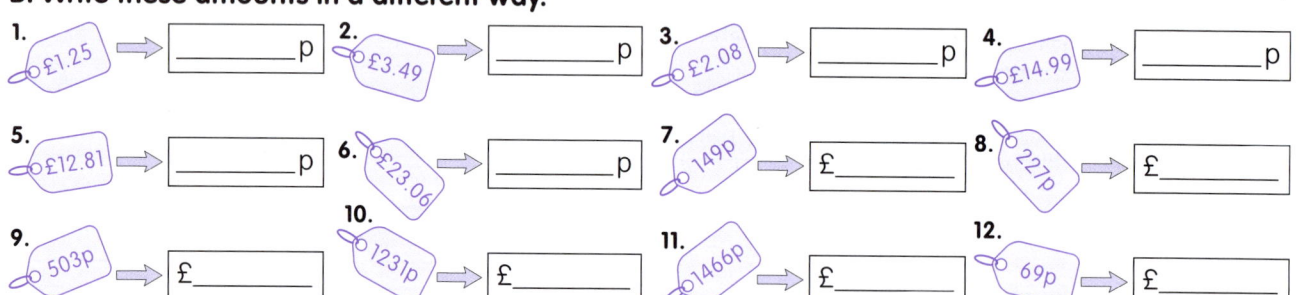

1. Change from	**£1**
48p →	
85p →	
37p →	
64p →	
91p →	
29p →	

2. Change from	**£5**
£4.30 →	
£2.89 →	
£3.21 →	
£4.06 →	
£2.97 →	
£1.84 →	

3. Change from	**£10**
£8.75 →	
£9.22 →	
£6.99 →	
£4.83 →	
£7.56 →	
£8.47 →	

Extension

D. Answer these problems.

1. Jo buys four pairs of socks at 80p a pair. How much change does she get from £5? _____

2. How many 8p sweets can David buy with 70p? _____

3. What is the total cost of four stamps at 30p and six stamps at 42p? _____

4. What is the change from £10 for six videos at £1.20 each? _____

5. Doughnuts cost £1.09 a pack. What is the cost of three packs? _____

6. CDs cost £7.49 in the sales. What change from £20 will there be for two CDs? _____

E. Answer these.

Cheese & Pickle **£1.24**

Sausage roll **63p** each

Samosa **38p** each

1. How much will three sausage rolls cost? _____

2. What is the total cost of a cheese & pickle sandwich and two sausage rolls? _____

3. How much will ten samosas cost? _____

4. What is the change from £5 for two cheese & pickle sandwiches and a samosa? _____

Challenge

F. A magazine costs £1.28.

The fewest coins needed to pay for it exactly is 5 coins.

£1.28 MAGAZINE OF THE MONTH

1. Write four other amounts that need exactly 5 coins.

   _____

2. Write four amounts that need exactly 6 coins.

   _____

3. What is the lowest amount that you can make with 6 different coins? _____

TOPIC 24: **Angles**

Focus

Angles are measures of turn. They are measured in **degrees**.

These are special angles to remember:

- A complete turn is 360° which is the same as four right angles.
- Half a complete turn is 180°. This looks like a straight line and is the same as two right angles.
- A quarter turn is 90°, also called a right angle.
- The three angles of an equilateral triangle 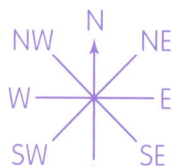 are 60° each.
- Half a right angle is 45°.

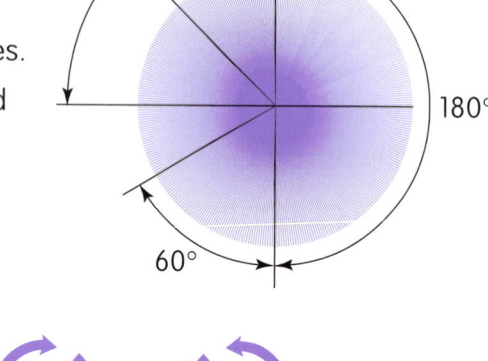

There are eight compass directions:

North, North-east, East, South-east, South, South-west, West, North-west

clockwise   anticlockwise

Practice

A. These angles show either 360°, 180°, 90°, 60° or 45°.

Write the size of each angle.

1. _____
2. _____
3. _____

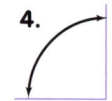
4. _____

5. _____

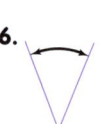
6. _____

7. _____

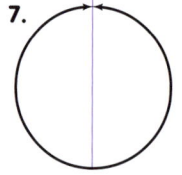
8. _____

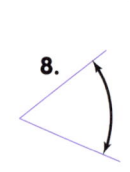
9. _____

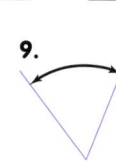
10. _____

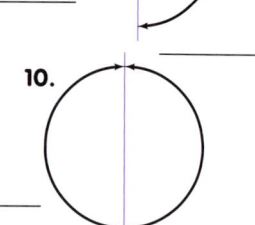

B. Write where you will face after each turn.

Face North to start each time

1. Make a 180° turn clockwise. _____
2. Make a 90° turn anticlockwise. _____
3. Make a 45° turn clockwise. _____

Face East to start each time

7. Make a 360° turn anticlockwise. _____
8. Make a 90° turn clockwise. _____
9. Make a 45° turn anticlockwise. _____

Face South to start each time

4. Make a 90° turn anticlockwise. _____
5. Make a 45° turn clockwise. _____
6. Make a 180° turn clockwise. _____

Face West to start each time

10. Make a 180° turn clockwise. _____
11. Make a 45° turn clockwise. _____
12. Make a 90° turn anticlockwise. _____

Extension

C. Tick the right angles on these shapes.

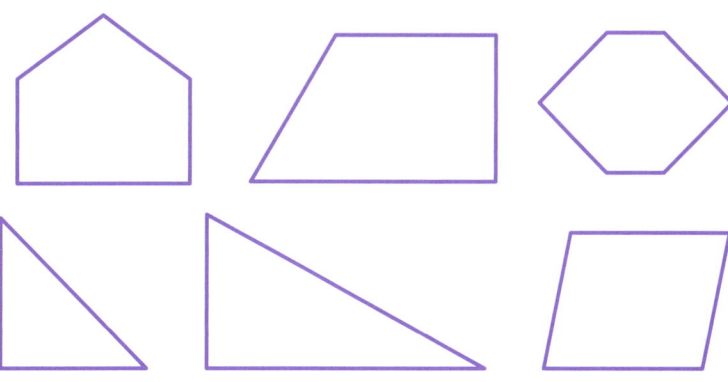

How many right angles are there altogether? ☐

D. Write these angles in order of size, starting with the smallest.

A 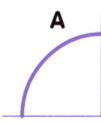 B 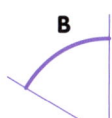 C 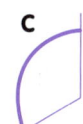 D 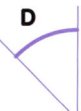 E  F

_____ _____ _____   _____ _____ _____

Challenge

E. Look at this dial from a washing machine.

The arrow turns clockwise.

Answer these questions.

1. How many degrees does the arrow turn from:

    pre-wash to spin _____

    wash to rinse _____

    rinse to off _____

    pre-wash to dry _____

2. Write the position the arrow is pointing to after these turns:

    60° from pre-wash _____

    120° from spin _____

    180° from wash _____

    360° from off _____

57

TEST 4 (Score 1 mark for every correct answer.)

Topic 19

1. Write these as decimals.

$\frac{3}{10}$ = ☐ $\frac{1}{2}$ = ☐

2. Write the decimals on this line.

☐ ☐

0 ├─┼─┼─┼─┼─┼─┼─┼─┼─┼─┤ 1

3. What is the value of the digit 5 in this number?

12.57 ☐

4. Write the correct signs < or > for these.

4.6 __ 4.8 __ 4.3

Topic 20

5. Write the missing amount.

$3\frac{1}{10}$ l = _____ ml

6. Write this as litres and millilitres.

4805 ml = _____ l _____ ml

7. How much liquid is in this jug?

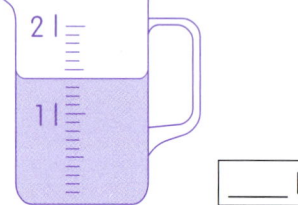

_____ l _____ ml

8. What is the difference between these two readings? ☐

Topic 21

9. Circle $\frac{1}{3}$ of the stars and write the answer.

$\frac{1}{3}$ of 12 = ☐

10. What is one-fifth of 30? ☐

11. What fraction of £2 is 50p? ☐

12. What fraction of 1 kilogram is 750 g? ☐

Topic 22

This bar chart shows the results of a survey of the types of pets owned by a group of people.

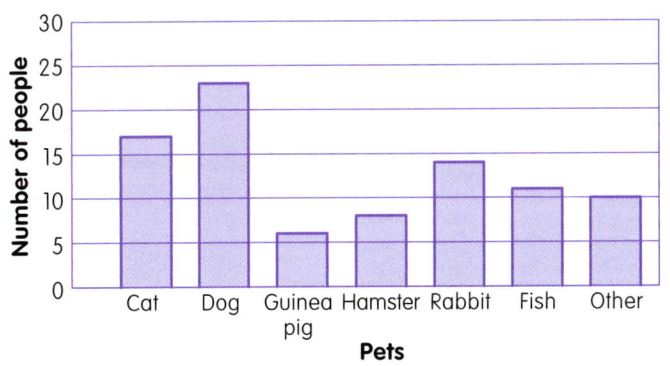

Use the graph to answer these questions.

13. How many people had a dog as a pet? ☐

14. Which type of pet was owned by 14 people? ☐

15. How many more people owned a cat than a fish? ☐

16. How many guinea pigs and hamsters were there in total? ☐

Topic 23

17. Write the total.

☐ p

18. Write these amounts.

£3.76 = _____ p   1245p = £ _____

19. A T-shirt costs £6.89. What change would be given from £10? ☐

20. Harry bought six felt-pens for 96p. How much would two felt-pens cost? ☐

Topic 24

21. Write the size of this angle.

_____ °

22. Tick the angle that shows 60°.

23. If you are facing North and turn anticlockwise by 45°, which direction will you now be facing? _____

24. Tick the right angles on this shape.

Mark the test. Remember to fill in your score on page 3.

Write your score out of 24. ☐

Add a BONUS POINT if you scored 20 or more.

TOTAL SCORE FOR TEST 4 ☐

How did you find the test?

Colour a face

too hard   too easy   about right

Answers

TOPIC 1: **Place value** (page 4)

A
1. 2100   6. 4935
2. 9184   7. 8057
3. 1480   8. 6092
4. 6206   9. 3001
5. 5680   10. 1009

B
1. 600
2. 100 + 40 + 5
3. 3000 + 200 + 90 + 8
4. 6000
5. 9000 + 300 + 7
6. 9000 + 800 + 30 + 4
7. 400 + 90
8. 500 + 90 + 8
9. 4000 + 600 + 80 + 9
10. 7000 + 90 + 4
11. 5000 + 800 + 90
12. 2000 + 900 + 40 + 6

C
1. 3099, 3248, 4769, 4796, 4966
2. 3080, 3445, 3546, 3550, 4992
3. 6009, 6097, 6109, 6977, 7102
4. 4020, 4200, 4399, 4559, 4560
5. 8090, 8329, 8392, 8900, 8932
6. 5002, 5020, 5022, 5202, 5222

D
1. 40   7. 40,000
2. 2000   8. 50
3. 6000   9. 6000
4. 600   10. 90
5. 80,000   11. 10,000
6. 50,000   12. 20

E
Check the ten numbers use each digit only once and that a number is not repeated.

Check the numbers are listed in order starting with the smallest.

TOPIC 2: **Addition facts** (page 6)

A

1. 11	2. 14	3. 19	4. 20
10	14	19	19
14	10	25	28
11	13	16	21
16	12	21	23
12	17	25	22
11	10	22	23
18	11	18	23
12	13	24	25
14	9	24	27

B
1. 60
   120
2. 40
3. 70
4. 30
5. 80
6. 50
7. 20
8. 90
9. 10

C
1. 110   3. 800
120   1300
130   1100
120   1500
120   1400
2. 130   4. 800
110   1100
150   1100
140   1300
140   1700

D

1. 14	3. 16	5. 13
24	26	23
34	36	33
44	46	43
54	56	53
2. 17	4. 15	6. 18
27	25	28
37	35	38
47	45	48
57	55	58

E
1. 15   9. 61
2. 1100   10. 41
3. 90   11. 170
4. 25   12. 27
5. 21   13. 26
6. 900   14. 34
7. 100   15. 1200
8. 27

F

1.
IN	4	8	1	7	13	11	7	14
OUT	23	**27**	20	**26**	32	**30**	26	**33**

2.
IN	4	7	9	16	13	15	18	23
OUT	13	**16**	18	**25**	22	**24**	27	**32**

3.
IN	3	6	2	10	8	12	11	9
OUT	32	**35**	31	**39**	37	**41**	40	**38**

TOPIC 3: **Subtraction facts** (page 8)

A

1. 11	2. 10	3. 16	4. 28
7	6	23	28
7	9	17	28
8	9	17	25
11	9	17	32
15	9	21	28
8	5	18	24
6	14	21	29
13	8	16	29
8	8	18	29

B
1. 50   3. 300
30   400
30   500
10   300
40   300
2. 130   4. 1500
70   1100
40   1100
80   300
120   700

C

1. 5	2. 6	3. 3	4. 6
9	8	8	9
7	9	10	5
8	10	6	7
10	13	14	15
4	15	17	12

D
1. 8   7. 8
2. 50   8. 40
3. 5   9. 7
4. 30   10. 400
5. 8   11. 11
6. 70   12. 500

E
1. 20, 6
2. 80, 10, 4
3. 75, 60, 15
4. 95, 40, 5

TOPIC 4: **Length** (page 10)

A
1. 5 km   9. 2 m
2. 10 km   10. 70 mm
3. 3.5 km   11. 6.5 m
4. 0.5 km   12. 635 cm
5. 6000 m   13. 4 cm
6. 20 m   14. 1200 m
7. 7500 m   15. 1.5 m
8. 5.25 m   16. 17.45 m

B
1. 6 cm
4 cm
5 cm
3 cm
2. 4.5 cm, 45 mm
2.5 cm, 25 mm
6.5 cm, 65 mm
5.5 cm, 55 mm

C
1. 65 mm
2. 55 mm
3. 75 mm
4. 43 mm

D
1. 35 cm
2. 9 km
3. 5.5 km
4. 1 m 60 cm
5. 700 cm
6. 230 km

E
1. 3 cm
2. 12 cm
3. 4.5 cm
4. 13.5 cm
5. 8 cm
6. 5 cm

TOPIC 5: **Multiplication and division facts** (page 12)

A
1. $5 \times 7 = 35$ $7 \times 5 = 35$ $35 \div 5 = 7$ $35 \div 7 = 5$
2. $9 \times 4 = 36$ $4 \times 9 = 36$ $36 \div 9 = 4$ $36 \div 4 = 9$
3. $6 \times 3 = 18$ $3 \times 6 = 18$ $18 \div 6 = 3$ $18 \div 3 = 6$
4. $5 \times 6 = 30$ $6 \times 5 = 30$ $30 \div 5 = 6$ $30 \div 6 = 5$
5. $9 \times 3 = 27$ $3 \times 9 = 27$ $27 \div 9 = 3$ $27 \div 3 = 9$
6. $7 \times 6 = 42$ $6 \times 7 = 42$ $42 \div 7 = 6$ $42 \div 6 = 7$
7. $9 \times 8 = 72$ $8 \times 9 = 72$ $72 \div 9 = 8$ $72 \div 8 = 9$
8. $6 \times 8 = 48$ $8 \times 6 = 48$ $48 \div 6 = 8$ $48 \div 8 = 6$

B

1. 45	2. 18	3. 7	4. 6
24	42	3	4
64	20	5	7
27	32	5	4
24	49	3	7
24	21	6	2
30	40	9	4
81	36	6	4
45	72	9	6
48	28	6	7

C

1.
IN	4	**3**	7	**9**	5	**8**
OUT	**24**	18	**42**	54	**30**	48

2.
IN	**5**	6	**2**	7	**9**	4
OUT	45	**54**	18	**63**	81	**36**

3.
IN	28	**12**	36	**32**	16	**20**
OUT	**7**	3	**9**	8	**4**	5

4.
IN	**18**	21	**27**	15	**12**	24
OUT	6	**7**	9	**5**	4	**8**

D

1.
x	6	8	4
3	18	**24**	**12**
9	**54**	**72**	36
2	**12**	**16**	8

2.
x	4	9	3
8	**32**	**72**	24
7	**28**	**63**	21
5	**20**	45	15

3.
x	4	6	7
2	**8**	**12**	14
5	**20**	**30**	35
8	**32**	**48**	56

4.
x	4	5	8
2	8	10	**16**
3	12	**15**	24
6	**24**	30	**48**

5.
x	3	7	9
4	**12**	28	36
7	21	**49**	63
8	24	56	**72**

6.
x	4	6	**10**
3	12	18	30
5	20	**30**	50
10	40	60	100

Topic 6: **2D shapes** (page 14)

A

1. triangle (regular)
2. triangle
3. rectangle or quadrilateral
4. hexagon (regular)
5. hexagon
6. triangle
7. square or rectangle or quadrilateral (regular)
8. quadrilateral
9. pentagon (regular)
10. quadrilateral
11. pentagon
12. octagon
13. decagon
14. nonagon
15. octagon (regular)

B

1. pentagons
2. quadrilaterals
3. heptagons
4. triangles
5. nonagons
6. octagons

C

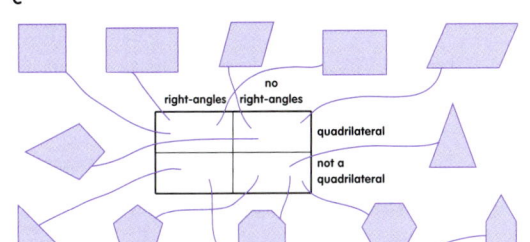

TEST 1 (page 16)

1. 6047
2. 7000 + 200
3. 6047, 6704, 6740, 7064, 7604
4. 60,000

5. 8
6. 120
7. 14, 24, 34
8. 20

9. 13
10. 900
11. 16
12. 70

13. 8 cm, 6.5 km
14. 3.5 cm, 35 mm
15. 7.5 cm
16. 8 cm

17. $8 \times 4 = \mathbf{32}$ $4 \times 8 = 32$ $\mathbf{32} \div 4 = \mathbf{8}$ $32 \div 8 = 4$
18. 42, 8

19.
IN	4	7	**6**	**9**	8	**2**
OUT	**32**	**56**	48	72	**64**	16

20.
x	3	8	**7**
4	**12**	**32**	**28**
6	**18**	48	**42**
9	**27**	**72**	63

21. pentagons

22. rectangle and quadrilateral
23. The pentagon is the odd one out; all the others are hexagons.
24. The two bottom corners are right angles.

TOPIC 7: **Time** (page 18)

A

1. 7.20
2. 4.15
3. 6.55
4. 10.40
5. 8.17
6. 12.37
7. 5.03
8. 9.29

B

1.
2.
3.
4.

C

Church Street	8.50am	9.35am	11.00am	1.05pm
Marsh Lane	9.15am	**10.00am**	**11.25am**	**1.30pm**
Hospital	**9.40am**	10.25am	11.50am	**1.55pm**
Swimming pool	**10.05am**	10.50am	**12.15pm**	2.20pm

D

1. 8.05pm
2. 1 hour and 25 minutes
3. 1.15pm
4. 1.25pm
5. 6 hours and 5 minutes

E

1. 20 minutes slow
2. 40 minutes slow
3. 4 minutes slow
4. 16 minutes slow
5. 55 minutes slow
6. 36 minutes slow

TOPIC 8: **Fractions of shapes** (page 20)

A

1. $\frac{1}{4}$
2. $\frac{1}{3}$
3. $\frac{1}{8}$
4. $\frac{1}{5}$
5. $\frac{1}{10}$
6. $\frac{1}{6}$
7. $\frac{2}{5}$
8. $\frac{3}{4}$
9. $\frac{3}{8}$
10. $\frac{4}{5}$
11. $\frac{9}{10}$
12. $\frac{4}{5}$

B

1. $\frac{1}{3} = \frac{2}{6}$
2. $\frac{1}{2} = \frac{6}{12}$
3. $\frac{1}{5} = \frac{3}{15}$
4. $\frac{1}{4} = \frac{4}{16}$
5. $\frac{1}{2} = \frac{5}{10}$
6. $\frac{1}{4} = \frac{3}{12}$

C

1. $\frac{1}{3}$
2. $\frac{3}{4}$
3. $\frac{1}{2}$
4. $\frac{1}{5}$
5. $\frac{3}{5}$
6. $\frac{1}{4}$

D

1. Any 3 boxes should be shaded.
2. Any 2 boxes should be shaded.
3. Any 4 boxes should be shaded.
4. Any 4 boxes should be shaded.
5. Any 2 boxes should be shaded.
6. Any 3 boxes should be shaded.

E

$\frac{1}{12}$ $\frac{1}{6}$ $\frac{1}{4}$ $\frac{1}{3}$ $\frac{1}{2}$ $\frac{2}{3}$ $\frac{3}{4}$ $\frac{5}{6}$

TOPIC 9: **Addition** (page 22)

A

1. 110
2. 85
3. 60
4. 120
5. 115
6. 90
7. 130
8. 125
9. 100
10. 100
11. 105
12. 130

B

1. 95
2. 115
3. 123
4. 98
5. 157
6. 76
7. 88
8. 79
9. 90
10. 89
11. 92
12. 82
13. 91
14. 91
15. 81
16. 126
17. 147
18. 131
19. 141
20. 142

C

1.
53	47	**100**
28	31	**59**
81	**78**	**318**

2.
31	67	**98**
42	39	**81**
73	**106**	**358**

3.
62	57	**119**
38	29	**67**
100	**86**	**372**

4.
62	53	**115**
74	47	**121**
136	**100**	**472**

D

74 → 37
68 → 43
67 → 44
47 → 64
78 → 33
57 → 54

E

1. 28 + **67** = 9**5**
2. 59 + **74** = 1**33**
3. **8**1 + 64 = 145

TOPIC 10: **Subtraction** (page 24)

A

1. 38 6. 28
2. 37 7. 26
3. 24 8. 29
4. 24 9. 17
5. 17 10. 35

B

1. 21 6. 34 11. 36 16. 37
2. 33 7. 27 12. 17 17. 27
3. 22 8. 47 13. 25 18. 39
4. 44 9. 38 14. 27 19. 25
5. 34 10. 55 15. 38 20. 26

C

1. 18 5. 28
2. 16 6. 17
3. 9 7. 16
4. 16 8. 25

D

83 → 39
62 → 18
93 → 49
52 → 96
33 → 77
53 → 97

E

1. 8**3** – **5**7 = 26 2. 9**4** – **6**8 = 26 3. **7**4 – 4**8** = 26

TOPIC 11: **Sequences and patterns** (page 26)

A

1. 15 3. 125 5. 65 7. 26 9. 43
   17   127   60   29   40
   19   129   55   32   37

2. 27 4. 270 6. 500 8. 18 10. 160
   32   280   400   22   150
   37   290   300   26   140

B

1. 24 3. 410 5. 99 7. 82 9. 47
   30   460   101   46   62
   36   710   109   28   65

2. 83 4. 38 6. 120 8. 89 10. 710
   58   46   125   73   510
   53   50   135   69   310

C

1. –5, –4, 1, 2
2. –25, –20, 5, 10
3. –6, –5, 0, 1
4. –18, –15, 0, 3
5. –14, –12, –2, 0
6. –10, –7, 8, 11
7. –11, –9, 1, 3
8. –18, –14, 6, 10

D

1. 35, 30
2. 31, 27
3. 43, 49
4. 468, 476
5. 910, 940
6. 144, 148

E

1	2	3	4	5	6	7	8
9	10	11	12	13	14	15	16
17	18	19	20	21	22	23	24
25	26	27	28	29	30	31	32
33	34	35	36	37	38	39	40
41	42	43	44	45	46	47	48
49	50	51	52	53	54	55	56
57	58	59	60	61	62	63	64

TOPIC 12: **Comparing and ordering numbers** (page 28)

A

1. 306, 368, 380, 800, 806, 860
2. 405, 450, 486, 589, 590, 594
3. 659, 689, 690, 906, 965, 966
4. 205, 215, 505, 512, 520, 522
5. 2599, 3005, 3125, 3152, 3502
6. 1670, 1706, 5799, 7509, 7611
7. 8079, 8095, 8307, 8345, 8543
8. 7244, 7323, 7324, 7332, 7342

B

1. < 6. <
2. < 7. >
3. > 8. >
4. > 9. <
5. > 10. <

C

1. 685 6. 1060
2. 4050 7. 390
3. 530 8. 6475
4. 5690 9. 720
5. 860 10. 8340

D

1. < >
2. > >
3. < <
4. > <
5. < >
6. > >

E

Island	Area (sq km)
Great Britain	218,041
Iceland	103,000
Ireland	83,766
Sicily	25,400
Sardinia	23,800
Cyprus	9251
Corsica	8270
Crete	8260

TEST 2 (page 30)

1. 6.12
2.

5. $\frac{3}{5}$
6. $\frac{1}{4} = \frac{2}{8}$
7. $\frac{1}{8}$
8. Any 6 boxes should be shaded

3. 50 minutes
4. 9.00

9. 165
10. 152
11.

53	47	**100**
28	31	**59**
81	**78**	**318**

12. 67 and 58

13. 38
14. 28
15. 45 and 93
16. 7**2** – **4**6 = 26

17. 28 and 33
18. 52 and 34
19. –14, –11, 4, 7
20. 37 and 41

21. 4679, 4767, 4769, 4799, 7649, 7697
22. 6105 < 6150
    4355 > 4335
23. 4220
24. 6104 > 3259 < 3260

TOPIC 13: **Rounding numbers** (page 32)

A

1. 460 7. 1470
2. 280 8. 9280
3. 150 9. 6960
4. 310 10. 3050
5. 640 11. 7650
6. 840 12. 9220

B

1. 700 7. 4900
2. 500 8. 7800
3. 100 9. 7700
4. 600 10. 4100
5. 800 11. 4000
6. 900 12. 2700

C

1. £1 7. £13
2. £5 8. £16
3. £2 9. £23
4. £6 10. £39
5. £5 11. £42
6. £9 12. £74

D

These are estimates.

1. 20 50 70 90
2. 50 80 150 250
3. 60 90 130 180
4. 120 200 400 480

E

These are estimates.

1. 200 400 700 900
2. 600 800 2300 2700
3. 500 900 1400 1800
4. 800 1900 3300 4700

F

These are estimates.

1. 380   2. 5900
   740   9600
   170   2600
   410   3300
   600   80,000
   1000   200,000

TOPIC 14: **Weight and mass** (page 34)

A

1. 2500 g
2. 3250 g
3. 750 g
4. 1100 g
5. 10,500 g
6. 2750 g
7. 6500 g
8. 12,750 g

B

1. 2 kg 400 g
2. 1 kg 700 g
3. 3 kg 550 g
4. 5 kg 850 g
5. 1 kg 20 g
6. 4 kg 230 g
7. 6 kg 125 g
8. 1 kg 875 g

C

1. 3 kg 500 g
2. 2 kg 500 g
3. 5 kg 500 g
4. 8 kg
5. 9 kg 600 g
6. 3 kg 900 g

D

1. 2 kg
2. 300 g
3. E
4. 50 g
5. 800 g
6. D and F

E

1. 4700 g
2. 5700 g
3. 2700 g
4. 2100 g
5. 4500 g
6. 3200 g

TOPIC 15: **3D shapes** (page 36)

A
1. cone
2. tetrahedron
3. sphere
4. hemisphere
5. cube
6. square based pyramid
7. cylinder

B
1. Cube – all the others are cuboids
2. Cone – all the others are cylinders
3. Square based pyramid – all the others are prisms
4. Prism – all the others are pyramids
5. Hemisphere – all the others are spheres

C
1. 1 square face and 4 triangular faces
2. 2 triangular faces and 3 rectangular faces
3. 2 square faces and 4 rectangular faces
4. 4 triangular faces

D
1. cube
2. tetrahedron
3. cuboid
4. hemisphere

TOPIC 16: **Multiplication** (page 38)

A
1. 60
2. 120
3. 200
4. 210
5. 120
6. 250
7. 540
8. 270
9. 320
10. 140
11. 240
12. 140
13. 240
14. 360
15. 240

B
1. 28
2. 34
3. 38
4. 46
5. 62
6. 56
7. 86
8. 94
9. 320
10. 500
11. 740
12. 980

C
1. 180
2. 69
3. 185
4. 72
5. 210
6. 153
7. 315
8. 116
9. 256
10. 165
11. 276
12. 370
13. 172
14. 237
15. 352

D
1. 258
2. 168
3. 98
4. 320
5. £152
6. 198

E
1. 288
2. 371
3. 414
4. 468
5. 476
6. 632

F
1. $23 \times 6 = 138$
2. $45 \times 7 = 315$
3. $68 \times 9 = 612$

TOPIC 17: **Division** (page 40)

A
1. 8
2. 9
3. 9
4. 10
5. 7
6. 12
7. 7
8. 16
9. 15
10. 18
11. 24
12. 19
13. 17
14. 13
15. 23

B
1. 17
2. 21
3. 19
4. 23
5. 16
6. 24
7. 28
8. 32
9. 41
10. 38
11. 47
12. 39

C
1. 8 r 3
2. 8 r 2
3. 23 r 1
4. 14 r 2
5. 10 r 2
6. 23 r 2
7. 41 r 1
8. 14 r 3
9. 14 r 4
10. 28 r 1
11. 14 r 5
12. 9 r 2
13. 10 r 6
14. 13 r 3
15. 16 r 2

D
1. 15
2. 49
3. 9
4. 14p
5. 11
6. 12

E
$56 \div 6 \rightarrow 2$
$71 \div 8 \rightarrow 7$
$96 \div 5 \rightarrow 1$
$86 \div 8 \rightarrow 6$
$77 \div 9 \rightarrow 5$
$99 \div 10 \rightarrow 9$
$89 \div 9 \rightarrow 8$
$52 \div 7 \rightarrow 3$
Check that the remainder for the child's own division is 4.

F
1. $75 \div 3 = 25$
2. $92 \div 2 = 46$
3. $12 \div 2 = 6$

TOPIC 18: **Coordinates** (page 42)

A
A = (3, 2)   F = (2,3)   D= (8,4)   H = (10,4)
(5, 5) = B   (0, 6) = G   (4, 8) = E   (1, 7) = C

B
Check coordinates are plotted correctly.

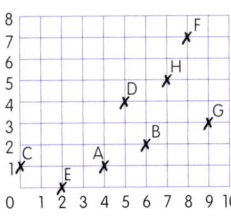

C

D
Check child's coordinates are correct for the star drawn.

E
1. A = (1, 3)
   B = (3, 1)
   C = (6, 4)
2. D = (4, 6)
3. Check corner D has been drawn in correctly at (4, 6).

TEST 3 (page 44)

1. 540, 6450
2. 800, 3100
3. £4, £25
4. 80, 130, 150, 180 (these are estimates)
5. 8100 g
6. 6 kg 225 g
7. 6 kg 700 g
8. 3 kg 0 g
9. hemisphere
10. The odd one out is the pentagonal prism; all the others are cuboids.
11. 2 hexagon faces and 6 rectangular faces
12. square based pyramid
13. 280
14. 112
15. 249
16. 150
17. 16
18. 38
19. 19 r 2
20. 16p
21. (4, 0)
22. C
23. (6, 3)
24. Check the child's cross is correctly placed at (3, 5).

TOPIC 19: **Decimals** (page 46)

A
1. 0.3
2. 0.9
3. 0.7
4. 0.5
5. 0.4
6. 0.8
7. 4.5
8. 2.1
9. 3.7
10. 5.3
11. 6.9
12. 4.2

B
1. 0.3, 0.5, 0.6, 0.9
2. 0.1, 0.4, 0.7, 0.8
3. 1.2, 1.4, 1.5, 1.7
4. 2.1, 2.3, 2.6, 2.9
5. 3.2, 3.5, 3.7, 3.8
6. 0.2, 0.6, 1.4, 1.8

C
1. $\frac{3}{10}$
2. $\frac{8}{10}$
3. $\frac{5}{100}$
4. $\frac{2}{100}$
5. $\frac{3}{10}$
6. $\frac{7}{100}$
7. $\frac{6}{10}$
8. $\frac{5}{100}$
9. $\frac{8}{10}$
10. $\frac{4}{10}$

D
1. <
2. >
3. >
4. >
5. <
6. <
7. <
8. >

E
1. 0.9, 2.9, 3, 3.1, 3.6, 3.8, 4
2. 0.4, 0.8, 4, 4.8, 8.1, 8.3, 8.32
3. 2, 2.1, 2.6, 2.71, 2.93, 7.17, 7.6
4. 3, 3.06, 10, 10.14, 10.35, 10.4, 11.1

TOPIC 20: **Capacity** (page 48)

A
1. 1500 ml
2. 2250 ml
3. 250 ml
4. 2100 ml
5. 6500 ml
6. 4750 ml
7. 8500 ml
8. 12,300 ml

B
1. 4 l 300 ml
2. 1 l 900 ml
3. 6 l 550 ml
4. 2 l 350 ml
5. 2 l 20 ml
6. 6 l 730 ml
7. 4 l 525 ml
8. 1 l 975 ml

C
1. 700 ml
2. 400 ml
3. 100 ml
4. 900 ml
5. 800 ml
6. 1200 ml
7. 1600 ml
8. 1800 ml
9. 1500 ml
10. 1300 ml

D
1. 1.5 l or 1½ l
2. 400 ml
3. C
4. 50 ml
5. 550 ml
6. F and D

E
1. 2800 ml
2. 4800 ml
3. 3700 ml
4. 4100 ml
5. 3900 ml
6. 5300 ml

TOPIC 21: **Fractions of amounts** (page 50)

A
1. 3
   5
   4
   6
2. 2
   4
   1
   3

B
1. 5
   4
   7
   6
   10
2. 4
   3
   6
   8
   5
3. 5
   8
   6
   10
   9
4. 3
   8
   7
   6
   10

C
1. $\frac{1}{2}$ $\frac{1}{5}$ $\frac{1}{10}$ $\frac{1}{4}$ $\frac{3}{4}$
2. $\frac{1}{10}$ $\frac{1}{2}$ $\frac{1}{4}$ $\frac{3}{4}$ $\frac{1}{5}$
3. $\frac{1}{4}$ $\frac{1}{2}$ $\frac{1}{10}$ $\frac{3}{4}$ $\frac{1}{5}$

D
1. $\frac{1}{10}$ $\frac{4}{10}$ or $\frac{2}{5}$ $\frac{2}{10}$ or $\frac{1}{5}$ $\frac{1}{2}$ $\frac{3}{10}$
2. $\frac{1}{4}$ $\frac{3}{4}$ $\frac{6}{10}$ or $\frac{3}{5}$ $\frac{8}{10}$ or $\frac{4}{5}$ $\frac{7}{10}$
3. $\frac{1}{2}$ $\frac{1}{4}$ $\frac{1}{10}$ $\frac{3}{4}$ $\frac{2}{10}$ or $\frac{1}{5}$

E
Check that the triangles coloured are as follows

6 triangles red
4 triangles blue
2 triangles yellow
8 triangles green
3 triangles orange
1 triangle will be left white

TOPIC 22: **Graphs** (page 52)

A
1. 40
2. Friday
3. Tuesday and Sunday
4. 16–19
5. Wednesday and Thursday
6. 26
7. 48
8. The museum may be closed on Wednesdays.

B
1. 21
2. 4
3. Car
4. 22
5. 33
6. 95

C
1. 78
2. December
3. November
4. 105
5. September

D
Check that the graph has been completed correctly.
1. Chris
2. David
3. Eric
4. Chris, Fred, Eric, David, Alan, Ben

TOPIC 23: **Money** (page 54)

A
1. 40p
2. 73p
3. 33p
4. 20p
5. 81p
6. 90p
7. 57p
8. 70p
9. 74p
10. 72p

B
1. 125p
2. 349p
3. 208p
4. 1499p
5. 1281p
6. 2306p
7. £1.49
8. £2.27
9. £5.03
10. £12.31
11. £14.66
12. £0.69

C
1. 52p 2. 70p 3. £1.25
   15p £2.11 78p
   63p £1.79 £3.01
   36p 94p £5.17
   9p £2.03 £2.44
   71p £3.16 £1.53

D
1. £1.80
2. 8
3. £3.72
4. £2.80
5. £3.27
6. £5.02

E
1. £1.89
2. £2.50
3. £3.80
4. £2.14

F
1. Check which 5 coins add to each of the four amounts.
2. Check which 6 coins add to each of the four amounts.
3. Lowest possible amount with 6 different coins is
   88p → 1p + 2p + 5p + 10p + 20p + 50p coins

TOPIC 24: **Angles** (page 56)

A
1. 45°
2. 90°
3. 180°
4. 90°
5. 180°
6. 45°
7. 360°
8. 60°
9. 60°
10. 360°

B
1. S
2. W
3. NE
4. E
5. SW
6. N
7. E
8. S
9. NE
10. E
11. NW
12. S

C
There are 16 right angles altogether.

D
F, D, B, A, C, E

E
1. 180° 2. WASH
   60° OFF
   180° DRY
   240° OFF

TEST 4 (page 58)

1. 0.3, 0.5
2. 0.4, 0.7
3. $\frac{5}{10}$
4. 4.6 < 4.8 > 4.3
5. 3100 ml
6. 4 l 805 ml
7. 1 l 400 ml
8. 700 ml
9. 4
10. 6
11. $\frac{1}{4}$
12. $\frac{3}{4}$
13. 23
14. rabbit
15. 6
16. 14
17. 77p
18. 376p, £12.45
19. £3.11
20. 32p
21. 180°
22.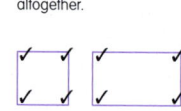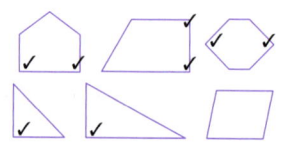
23. NW
24. All four corners should be ticked on the rectangle.